BASEBALL RULES IN PICTURES

G. JACOBS
&
J. R. McCRORY

with an introduction by Ron Luciano

A Perigee Book

DEDICATION

To C. O. Brown, late president of the American Amateur Baseball Congress, who contributed his knowledge and advice to the preparation of this book as selflessly as he had devoted his life to amateur athletics on behalf of the youth of America.

Also gratefully acknowledged is the serving of George Barr, National League umpire for 20 years, and H. V. Porter, Former Executive Secretary of the National Federation of State High School Athletic Associations, as technical consultants.

The set of six film strips in color entitled **Baseball Rules and Officiating** from which this book was made is available from Teaching Aids Service, Inc., Visual Education Building, Lowell Avenue and Cherry Lane, Floral Park, Long Island, N. Y. 11001

Perigee Books
are published by
The Putnam Publishing Group
200 Madison Avenue
New York, NY 10016

Published simultaneously in Canada by
General Publishing Co. Limited, Toronto.

Library of Congress Cataloging in Publication Data

McCrory, G. Jacobs.
Baseball rules in pictures.

Summary: The rules of baseball presented in text
and illustrations. 1. Baseball—Rules. [1. Baseball—
Rules] I. McCrory, J. R. II. Title.
[GV877.M23   1985]   796.357'02'022   84-18973
ISBN 0-399-51129-6

PRINTED IN THE UNITED STATES OF AMERICA
7 8 9 10

INTRODUCTION

The man, or woman, on the field in charge of a baseball game is called the umpire. Of course, if he makes a questionable call against the home team on a play, he will be called many other things too. I was a major league umpire for eleven years, and I always called the plays as I saw them—when I saw them. Players and managers often questioned my eyesight, my judgment, even my sanity, but they never questioned my knowledge of the rules.

An umpire has to know the rulebook. His job depends on it. I found during my career that those players and managers who really knew the rules were able to take full advantage of a situation on the field. I've seen teams lose games because a player left a base earlier than permitted, or because a pitcher didn't realize he was committing a balk. And, in 1914, a team actually lost the pennant because a runner did not know he had to touch second base when the batter hit a single and a runner on third base scored the "winning" run.

The basic rules of baseball are not complicated. Perhaps the simplest explanation of the rules I have ever heard came from the grandmother of a childhood friend of mine. "One man throws the ball at another man," she said. "The other man tries to hit it with a stick. If he is able to hit it, he is so happy that he runs around like a crazy person!"

Actually, she almost had it right. Baseball is a game of throwing, hitting, catching, and running. And once you have mastered those skills, you will be able to play the game on any level. But as important as it is to be able to do those things, you must know the rules of the game.

When I was growing up in Endicott, New York, we had to make rules that conformed to our ballfield. If a ball rolled down a water-grate the batter was entitled to a double. If a ball went rolling down the hill, the last one down—the last player to get on his knees—had to get it. And finally, if it went anywhere near Biondo's Bakery, the place with the sweetest rolls and most delicious cakes I've ever tasted, I was not allowed to retrieve it.

But as I got older, and baseball fields became a little more uniform, I learned that a single set of rules governs all organized baseball. I liked that—unlike math, a subject in which every time I thought I'd learned it, they would add another rule or complication.

Knowing the rules will not help you hit a pitch farther or enable you to throw a better fastball. What it will do is give you the same opportunity to win as the most knowledgeable player on the field. The player who doesn't know the rules starts with a disadvantage that sometimes even talent isn't enough to overcome.

I think baseball is the most beautiful game there is to watch, and one of the most enjoyable to play. But to play it right, you have to know the game inside and out. So remember, learn the rules, keep your eye on the baseball, and please, please, never, ever argue with the umpire.

He's trying just as hard as you are—and he may be my relative.

Ron Luciano

FOREWORD

The crack of a bat, the thump of a baseball in a mitt, the shouts of happy youngsters have long been familiar summer sounds in vacant lots all over America. In recent years thousands of these boys have received the opportunity to play in organized amateur leagues, properly planned, equipped, coached, and supervised.

In the youngest program organized on a national basis, the Little Leagues, there are approximately a million participants. Figures from the office of the Commissioner of Baseball indicate that the grand total of participants rises to over 6,000,000 if we include other programs such as the Babe Ruth League, Boys Baseball (Bronco-Pony-Colt), The American Legion program, the Connie Mack and the Stan Musial Divisions of the American Amateur Baseball Congress, and the thousands of unaffiliated playground and sandlot, college and high school teams, the Junior Chamber of Commerce program, the Little Pacific Coast League, the Young America League, Teener League, National Junior League and others.

For all these youngsters, for their coaches, umpires, managers, and for interested parents, certainly the basis for enjoying the game is an understanding of the rules of baseball, and the same is obviously true for the fans of professional baseball. For all these, this book offers a quick and easy way to learn the rules and to check on questions that may arise from the rules.

The plan of the book is simplicity itself. Nearly 200 clear pictures illustrate actual playing situations and the captions explain the rules involved. For those who want to check the wording of the rule itself, every caption is keyed to the Official Baseball Rules in the back of the book. The book is divided into four parts: The Pitcher, The Batter, The Runner, The Umpire. The selection from the Official Baseball Rules covers those rules that apply to all organized leagues with exceptions for Little Leagues noted. Matters of organization, equipment and the playing field are not covered since they vary among amateur leagues.

The pictures and captions are taken from an educational film strip prepared by Teaching Aids Service, Inc., which has been praised by teachers, coaches, professional umpires, and amateur league officials throughout the country.

Part 1: THE PITCHER

To begin play the umpire calls "Play!" while the pitcher is in the pitching position. (Rule 4.02)

SET POSITION

WIND UP POSITION

The pitcher may use one of two starting positions. Either is legal at any time.
(Rule 8.01 a-b)

WIND UP POSITION

The pitcher must stand squarely facing the batter, with his pivot foot ON or IN FRONT of the pitcher's plate. (Rule 8.01 a)

WIND UP POSITION   **NOT LIKE THIS**

The pivot foot must be touching. (Rule 8.01 a-b)

The pivot foot is RIGHT for the right-handed pitcher. (Rule 2.00)

The pivot foot is LEFT for the left-handed pitcher. (Rule 2.00)

SET POSITION

WIND UP POSITION

The pitcher's pivot foot must touch the rubber in either position. (Rule 8.01 a-b)

WIND UP POSITION

His other foot is free, but the pitcher must not raise either foot from the ground except to deliver the ball. (Rule 8.01 a)

WIND UP POSITION

STEP 2

STEP 1

He may take one step backward and one step forward with his free foot in pitching. (Rule 8.01 a)

In the set position the pitcher faces the batter sideways with ENTIRE pivot foot ON or IN FRONT OF and IN CONTACT with the rubber. (Rule 8.01 b)

SET POSITION

Pivot foot may NOT be off the end of the rubber. (Rule 8.01 b)

STARTING POSITION

In the set position, the pitcher must hold the ball with both hands in front of his body. (Rule 8.01 b)

SET POSITION

He may stretch and return, but must come to a complete stop before pitching.
(Rule 8.01 b)

SET POSITION

After taking the SET position, the pitcher may pitch to the batter—or
(Rule 8.01 b)

NOTE: The rules concerning a pitcher's throw to a base to catch a runner do not apply in Little League play, since the Little League rules require all runners to remain on base until the pitch has reached the batter.

SET POSITION

The pitcher may throw to a base—or (Rule 8.01 c)

FROM THE SET POSITION

The pitcher may step backward off rubber with pivot foot before "breaking" hands for actual pitch to batter or throw to base. (Rule 8.01 b)

If a pitcher throws to base, he must step directly toward that base. Penalty: Balk (Rule 8.01 c)

With no runner on base, pitcher must deliver ball within 20 seconds after receiving it. Penalty: Umpire calls "Ball" for each violation. This does not apply in Little League. (Rule 8.04)

He may not deface the ball in any way before pitching. Penalty: Eviction from game. (Rule 8.02 a; 3.02)

If there is a runner or runners, the pitcher, while touching his plate, may not throw, or feint a throw, to an unoccupied base, except for the purpose of making a play. Penalty: Balk (Rule 8.05 d)

The pitcher may not intentionally pitch at the batter. Penalty: Eviction from the game after a warning. (Rule 8.02 d)

A balk is an act by a pitcher to unfairly take advantage of, or to deceive, a runner. A balk pitch is not a ball or strike. (Penalty: If ball is not hit, award all runners one base advance.) A balk is not an appeal play. Umpire must call it immediately upon commission.

A BALK

Bluffing a pitch to batter, then throwing to 1st to catch runner. (Rule 8.05 a)

A BALK

Bluffing a throw to 1st and not completing it. (Pitcher may bluff to 2nd or 3rd without balking.) (Rule 8.05 b)

Pitcher making a motion associated with pitching to batter and failing to complete pitch. (Rule 8.05 a)

Throwing to any base to catch a runner without stepping directly toward that base. (Rule 8.05 c)

Pitcher taking position on or near rubber without the ball in his possession. (Rule 8.05 i)

NO. 1 FOR ALL BALKS

Penalty—if ball is hit fairly. When batter and runners advance at least one base safely—play stands—even if any runner is put out trying to advance further. (Rule 8.05)

NO. 2 FOR ALL BALKS

Go back!

Penalty—if ball is hit fairly. When batter and runners **DO NOT** advance at least one base safely—runners are given one base from original base held at balk. **Batter returns to bat.** (Rule 8.05)

A QUICK QUIZ

1. What is wrong here?

2. What is wrong here?

3. What is wrong here?

1. **The pitcher did not step toward 1st base as he threw the ball.** (Rule 8.01 c)

2. **Pitcher threw to unoccupied base, but not to make the play there.** (Rule 8.05 d)

3. **The pitcher does not have the ball and the pivot foot is not touching the rubber.** (Rule 8.05 i)

Part 2: THE BATTER

The batter must stand with both feet within the batter's box. (Rule 6.03)

The batter shall not leave his position in the batter's box after the pitcher comes to the "Set" position or starts his windup. Penalty: "Ball" or "Strike" as the case may be. (Rule 6.02 b)

He is OUT if he hits the ball with either foot entirely outside lines of batter's box. (Rule 6.06 a and Rule 2.00 ILLEGALLY BATTED BALL.)

Any ball at which he swings and misses is a STRIKE, regardless of position of pitch. (Rule 2.00)

It is a strike if a ball enters the STRIKE ZONE over home plate and the batte does not swing at it—even if it hits him. (Rule 2.00)

A pitch, OUTSIDE THE STRIKE zone, not swung at by the batter, is a BALL. (Rule 2.00)

FAIR BALL

A fair ball must:
- Settle in fair territory between first and third bases—or
- Bounce past third or first base in fair territory—or
- Bounce over first or third base—or
- Fall fair and roll foul beyond first or third base
- Be over fair territory when it passes out of playing field in flight

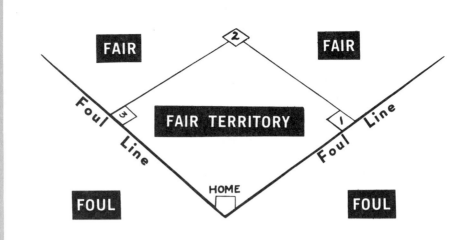

FAIR territory is territory within foul lines. FOUL territory is area outside the foul lines. (Rule 2.00)

THE RUNNER IS CALLED BACK

THE BALL IS DEAD

It is a fair ball if it strikes the umpire on fair territory—before touching a fielder or passing a fielder other than the pitcher. (Rule 2.00; 6.08 d)

THE BALL IS DEAD

It is a fair ball if it strikes a player on fair territory. Runner struck is out. Batter goes to first; others advance ONLY if forced. (Rule 2.00; 6.08 d)

A foul direct off the bat to the catcher and caught is a **FOUL TIP** and is in play. If caught on rebound, **NOT A CATCH** unless ball touches catcher's glove or hand first. (Rule 2.00)

A batter may run when he hits a fair ball. (Rule 6.09 a)

A batter may run when he has three strikes—if the catcher fails to catch the ball, unless first base is occupied and there are less than 2 outs. This does not apply to Little Leagues. (Rule 6.09 b)

The batter is OUT if he hits a fair fly ball which is caught by a fielder before it touches the ground. (Rule 6.05 a)

The batter is out if he hits a foul fly ball which is caught by a fielder before it touches the ground. (Rule 6.05 a)

The batter is out if his third strike is caught by the catcher. (Rule 6.05 b)

The batter is also out after third strike not caught if less than two are out and a runner is on 1st. (Rule 6.05 c)

If the 3rd strike is not caught—with less than 2 out and 1st base is not occupied —the runner is safe if he can beat the throw to 1st. This does not apply to Little League. (Rule 6.09 b)

INFIELD FLY

An infield fly is a fair fly ball which can reasonably be handled by an infielder and which occurs when there are fewer than two outs and there are runners on first and second, whether or not there may also be a runner on third.

The umpire should call, "Infield fly; batter out if fair."

Runners advance at their own risk.

he batter is **OUT** on an infield fly; but a runner on his base struck by an infield fly is **NOT OUT.** (Rule 7.08 f)

"Rule of thumb" to determine if infield fly: Could fielder be facing toward batter when making catch? Here **NOT** an infield fly. (Rule 2.00)

The batter is out if he bunts the third strike foul. (Rule 6.05 d)

The batter is out if the third strike hits him. (Rule 6.05 f)

The batter is out if his fair hit ball bounces up and hits him before touching a fielder. (Rule 6.05 g)

The batter is out if the ball is held by a fielder on 1st base after a third strike —not caught. (Rule 6.05 j)

he batter is out if a fair hit ball is held by a fielder on first base before the batter reaches 1st. (Rule 6.05 j)

The batter is OUT if touched before he reaches 1st base on a fair hit ball, or on a 3rd strike which is not caught. (Rule 6.05 j)

THE BALL REMAINS IN PLAY

The batter is NOT out if he drops the bat and the ball rolls and hits the bat, unless the umpire judges act as intentional. (Rule 6.05 h)

The batter is out if he runs more than 3 feet out of the baseline to avoid being tagged. (Rule 7.08 a)

The batter is out if he interferes with a fielder. (Rule 6.05 k; 7.08 b)

A force out is made by tagging a base ahead of a runner only when he is forced to advance because batter becomes a runner. (Rule 7.08 e)

This situation is not a force play. First base is open for the batter.
(Rule 7.08 e)

Unless a force play, no runner can force another runner. He retains right to base. Man originally on 1st base must get back. (Rule 7.03)

The batter is out when an infielder intentionally drops a fly ball   (to make a force play possible).   (Rule 6.05 l)

A batter is out when an infielder intentionally drops a line drive   (in order to make a force play possible).   (Rule 6.05 l)

THE BALL IS DEAD

The batter is out when a runner interferes with a defensive player catching a thrown ball, or throwing to complete a play. Additional Penalty: Runners return.   (Rule 6.05 m)

The batter is out when a spectator clearly prevents a fielder from catching a fly ball. (Rule 3.16 APPROVED RULING)

The legal batter is out if someone else bats in his turn. Improper batter is not out. Appeal must be made to umpire by defensive team before the next play or attempted play. If not so appealed the play stands. Under High School rules, the scorer, umpire, or any offensive player may correct the infraction without penalty before the ball is pitched to improper batter.

The proper batter Number 2 comes to bat and assumes the ball and strike count of the improper batter Number 3. (Rule 6.07)

If an appeal is made after Number 3 has completed his time at bat and before the next pitch to batter, the next play or attempted play, Number 2 is out. Bases run and scores do not count. (Rule 6.07 b)

"Jeopardy" means in danger of being put out, as the ball is in play.

To be "awarded" a base means to be permitted to advance there without jeopardy—that is, without danger of being put out.

The batter is awarded 1st base by having 4 balls called by the umpire. (Rule 6.08 a)

THE BALL IS DEAD

The batter is awarded 1st base if catcher or any other fielder interferes with him unless his manager notifies umpire immediately that he wishes play to stand because it is to his advantage. (Rule 6.08 c)

THE BALL IS DEAD

The batter is awarded 1st base when a fair hit ball strikes the umpire before touching or passing a fielder, other than the pitcher. (Rule 6.08 d)

THE BALL IS DEAD

The batter is awarded 1st base when his fair hit ball strikes the runner before touching or passing a fielder, other than the pitcher. Runner is out. (Rule 6.08d; 7.08 f)

POW

THE BALL IS DEAD

The batter is awarded 1st base if struck by a pitched ball not in the strike zone which he is not attempting to hit and which he tries to avoid. (Rule 6.08 b)

If the batter does not try to avoid a pitched ball it is called ball or strike as the case may be. (Note to Rule 6.08 b)

The ball is dead on a foul fly not caught. Runners return. (Rule 5.09 e)

The ball is dead when a thrown ball or a fair hit ball goes into the stands. Runners advance. (Rule 7.05)

The ball is dead if a legally pitched ball hits a runner trying to score. Runners advance. (Rule 5.09 h)

Ball is dead if the umpire interferes with a catcher attempting to throw to catch runner. Runners return. (Rule 5.09 b)

DEAD BALL

When the ball is dead the play stops. No runs count and no one can advance—except as the result of acts while the ball was alive.
The most common exceptions are:

EXCEPTION 1

Overthrow into crowd. (Rule 7.05 g-h)

EXCEPTION 2

A Balk. (Rule 2.00; 7.04 a)

EXCEPTION 3

SOMETIMES on Obstruction or Interference, but only under circumstances described in these pictures.

EXCEPTION 4

Fair ball hit out of playing field. (Rule 7.05 a)

The pitcher puts the ball in play to resume the game—AFTER the umpire calls "Play!" The ball is now in play. (Rule 5.11)

A QUICK QUIZ

1. Is this bunt FAIR or FOUL?

2. Why isn't this an infield fly?

3 FT.

3. Why is the runner out?

4. Where is a force play possible?

5. What is wrong here?

6. What do you do with the runners here?

ANSWERS

1. **FAIR. It came back by 3rd base.** (Rule 2.00)

2. **Runner on first only when ball was hit.** (Rule 2.00)

3. **The runner ran more than 3 feet out of the baseline to avoid being tagged.** (Rule 7.08 a)

4. 2nd and 1st only. Runner on third not forced. (Rule 7.08 e)

5. Ball is dead. Runner on 2nd does not advance. (Rule 5.09 a)

6. Award batter 1st. Runner hit is out. Runner on 3rd does not advance—not forced to do so. (Rule 5.09 f; 7.08 f)

The runner must touch 1st, 2nd, 3rd and home bases in order to score a run.
(Rule 2.00; 7.02)

If forced to return, a runner must touch bases in reverse order—unless the ball is dead. (Rule 7.02)

Two runners may not occupy the same base. The first runner retains right to base, except on a force play. (Rule 7.01)

If not a force play, and a following runner is tagged while on base, he is out.
(Rule 7.03)

RUNNER ADVANCES

Runners advance one base without jeopardy when batter is awarded 1st base and runners must advance to open base for him. (Rule 7.04 b)

The runner is entitled to advance without jeopardy to base he is attempting to steal if catcher interferes with batter. (Rule 7.04 d)

If play is made on runner obstructed by a defensive player, ball is dead and he must be awarded at least one base. (Rule 7.06 a)

If no play is made on obstructed runner, play goes to completion and umpire imposes penalties, if necessary, to nullify obstruction. (Rule 7.06 b)

All runners and batter are entitled to advance home without jeopardy when a fair ball is hit over the fence. (Rule 7.05 a)

All runners and batter are entitled to advance home without jeopardy when ball is prevented from going over the fence by a fielder striking it with a thrown glove, apparel or equipment. (Rule 7.05 a)

All runners and batter advance 3 bases without jeopardy if a fielder touches any fair ball with a thrown mask, glove or detached part of uniform. Batter may try for home at his own risk. (Rule 7.05 b)

If a ball is thrown, not batted, and a fielder strikes it with a thrown glove or any other piece of equipment, runners and the batter advance 2 bases without jeopardy—more at own risk. (Rule 7.05 e)

The runner is awarded 2 bases, without jeopardy, from base occupied at time ball was pitched, if throw was first by an infielder unless runners had advanced at least one base at time throw was made. (Rule 7.05 g)

If a play intervenes between 1st throw by an infielder and throw into stands, if runners had advanced at least one base at time of throw or if the throw is made by a outfielder, two bases are awarded runners from base to which entitled at time of throw. (Rule 7.05 g)

A wild pitch to batter which goes into the stands, bench, etc., entitles runners to advance one base without jeopardy. (Rule 7.05 h)

When the runner on 3rd attempts to score on steal or squeeze bunt and catcher interferes with batter, award runner home, batter 1st. (Rule 7.07)

The runner is out when he fails to yield right of way to a fielder fielding a fair hit ball. (Rule 7.08 b)

The runner is out when he intentionally interferes with a thrown ball. (Rule 7.08 b)

The runner is out when he is tagged by a fielder while off base. (Rule 7.08 c)

The runner is out if he passes the preceding runner unless that runner has been put out as occurs occasionally on "run-down" plays. (Rule 7.08 h)

The runner is out when the base to which he is advancing on a force play is tagged. (Rule 7.08 e)

A runner is out when he is tagged with the ball on a force play. (Rule 7.08 e)

APPEAL PLAYS

An appeal must be made to the umpire by a defensive player before the next pitch to the batter, the next play or attempted play such as trying to catch a runner off base. (Rule 7.10)

An appeal is defined by the rules as the act of a fielder in claiming a violation of the rules by the offensive team. (Rule 2.00)

Hitting with an illegal bat (such as a loaded or deliberately flattened bat) is now an appeal play and batter is out on proper appeal after he hits with such a bat. (Rule 6.06 d and Rule 2.00 ILLEGALLY BATTED BALL.)

THIS IS AN APPEAL PLAY

If a runner leaves base before a fly ball, fair or foul, is caught, he is out if the base is tagged before his return to base. (Rule 7.08 d)

THIS IS AN APPEAL PLAY

If a runner leaves base before a fly ball, fair or foul, is caught, he is out if he is tagged before his return to base. (Rule 7.08 d)

THIS IS AN APPEAL PLAY

If a runner misses a base, he may be put out by a fielder touching the base with the ball before the runner retags the base. (Rule 7.10 b)

THIS IS AN APPEAL PLAY

Failing to return to 1st base immediately after overrunning or oversliding. (Rule 7.10 c)

THIS IS AN APPEAL PLAY

The runner is out if he overslides home plate—misses it—and the plate is tagged by a fielder before the runner returns. (Rule 7.10 d)

A baserunner must return to base on a foul ball not caught. Umpire shall not put ball in play until all runners have retouched their bases. (Rule 5.09 e)

The runner need not retouch after a foul tip as this is considered a regular strike. (Rule 2.00)

INTERFERENCE PLAYS

On all interference plays the ball is dead and runner returns to base occupied when ball was pitched.

INTERFERENCE

THE BALL IS DEAD. RUNNERS RETURN TO BASE

The batter interferes with play at plate. If less than 2 outs—the runner is out. If 2 are out—the batter is out. (Rule 7.08 g)

INTERFERENCE

THE BALL IS DEAD. RUNNERS RETURN TO BASE

The runner is out, if on third, and the coach leaves the coach's box to make movement intended to draw the throw from the fielder. (Rule 7.09 j)

INTERFERENCE

The runner is out if teammates gather around a base to which runner is advancing to confuse or hinder the defensive team. (Rule 7.09 e)

THESE RUNS SCORE

If a preceding runner "misses" a base, it does not affect the baserunners behind him, whether put out or not, unless it's the 3rd out. (Rule 7.12)

Runs score if appeal play for third out is behind runner unless it is a force out. (Rule 7.12)

If the batter is put out before reaching 1st. (Rule 4.09 a)

If any other runner is put out by a force out for 3rd out. (Rule 4.09 a)

If a preceding runner is the 3rd out on an appeal play. (Rule 4.09 a)

1. Where do you place the players?

2. The batter is hit by a pitched ball. What do you do with the runners?

3. What is your decision?

A QUICK QUIZ

4. What are baserunning appeal plays?

5. Does the second run count?

6. What is your decision?

1. Place runner on 3rd and 2nd. One cannot put two men on one base.
(CASEBOOK 7.05 g)

2. Advance runner on 1st to 2nd. Put batter on 1st. Hold runner on 3rd.
(Rule 7.04 b)

3. Wait until end of play since no play is made on obstructed runner. Then impose penalties to nullify act of obstruction, if necessary. (Rule 7.06)

THIS IS AN APPEAL PLAY

4-a. Missing a base. (Rule 7.10 b)

THIS IS AN APPEAL PLAY

4-b. Failing to re-tag a base after a fly is caught. (Rule 7.08 d; 7.10 a)

THIS IS AN APPEAL PLAY

4-c. Failing to return to 1st base immediately after overrunning or oversliding. (Rule 7.10 c)

THIS IS AN APPEAL PLAY.

4-d. Missing home plate. (Rule 7.10 d)

5.   NO. The run does NOT count if the appeal is third out. (Rule 4.09 a)

6.   Runner is out. Batter gets 1st base. (Any other runners return to base.)
(Rule 7.08 b)

Part 4: THE UMPIRE

See that the field is marked plainly. (Rule 3.01 b)

See that pitcher's rubber is in good condition. (Rule 3.01 a)

To be a good umpire is something to be proud of. It is not an easy job, but there is great satisfaction from doing it right. Of course you must know the game and you must keep alert; but beyond that you must be careful to keep your feelings in complete control. "Call the plays, never the players."

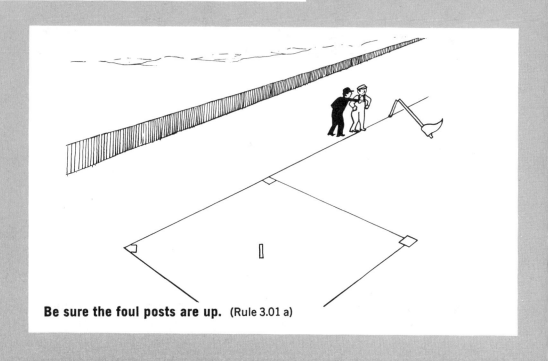

Be sure the foul posts are up. (Rule 3.01 a)

Receive batting orders in duplicate. Check to be sure they are identical. Give extra copy to opposing manager. (Rule 4.01 a-c)

Be in a position to call all plays. If working alone, start game behind the plate.

KEEP YOUR EYE ON THE BALL   HUSTLE

With a runner on 1st only, take position behind pitcher. Try not to "'shadow" the pitch to batter.

When there is one umpire, he remains behind the plate when there are runners on bases other than first.

KEEP YOUR EYE ON THE BALL

HUSTLE

15'

Most Amateur games use two umpires. One is always behind the plate. With nobody on base, the other umpire stands as shown.

KEEP YOUR EYE ON THE BALL

HUSTLE

On balls hit to second baseman he moves here.

3

KEEP YOUR EYE ON THE BALL

HUSTLE

On balls hit to shortstop or 3rd baseman he moves here.

BE IN A POSITION TO SEE EVERY PLAY

On other than tag plays, "Listen" for ball in glove, "Look" for tag of runner's foot and also try to catch ball out of the corner of your eye.

KEEP YOUR EYE ON THE BALL

HUSTLE

With runner on second, stand (R) for right-handed pitchers, (L) for left-handed pitchers to prevent "shadowing" the ball.

Bases full, with infield back, position is here.

With bases full and infield "in" go behind shortstop.

With runner on third only, one or none out, many umpires prefer this position.

The umpire's signal for a strike.

The umpire's signal for out.

The signal for safe.

"Balls" are not indicated, merely called vocally.

Call FOUL balls only when sure and when ball will be close. Do not call FAIR balls. Indicate by pointing whether ball is INSIDE or OUTSIDE the foul line.

Give balls on left hand, strikes on right every few pitches. It avoids unnecessary questions.

Don't "give away" appeal plays.

KEEP YOUR EYE ON THE BALL

Be in a position to see every play.

Don't call plays on the run. Set yourself.

KEEP YOUR EYE ON THE BALL   HUSTLE

Protect yourself on an infield fly. Always call "Infield fly, if fair."

To avoid arguments between innings, walk slightly from home plate toward bench of team going into field.

When anyone argues, listen briefly, say "I saw the play this way and that's it. Play ball." Then walk a few steps away.

KEEP YOUR EYE ON THE BALL

When cleaning home plate, step inside the diamond, face crowd, turn back to pitcher, lean over and brush plate. Keep plate clean.

2.00—Definitions of Terms.

(All definitions in Rule 2.00 are listed alphabetically.)

ADJUDGED is a judgment decision by the umpire.

An APPEAL is the act of a fielder in claiming violation of the rules by the offensive team.

A BALK is an illegal act by the pitcher with a runner or runners on base, entitling all runners to advance one base.

A BALL is a pitch which does not enter the strike zone in flight and is not struck at by the batter.

If the pitch touches the ground and bounces through the strike zone it is a "ball." If such a pitch touches the batter, he shall be awarded first base. If the batter swings at such a pitch after two strikes, the ball cannot be caught, for the purposes of Rule 6.05 (c) and 6.09 (b). If the batter hits such a pitch, the ensuing action shall be the same as if he hit the ball in flight.

A BASE is one of four points which must be touched by a runner in order to score a run; more usually applied to the canvas bags and the rubber plate which mark the base points.

A BASE COACH is a team member in uniform who is stationed in the coach's box at first or third base to direct the batter and the runners.

A BASE ON BALLS is an award of first base granted to a batter who, during his time at bat, receives four pitches outside the strike zone.

A BATTER is an offensive player who takes his position in the batter's box.

BATTER-RUNNER is a term that identifies the offensive player who has just finished his time at bat until he is put out or until the play on which he became a runner ends.

The BATTER'S BOX is the area within which the batter shall stand during his time at bat.

The BATTERY is the pitcher and catcher.

BENCH OR DUGOUT is the seating facilities reserved for players, substitutes and other team members in uniform when they are not actively engaged on the playing field.

A BUNT is a batted ball not swung at, but intentionally met with the bat and tapped slowly within the infield.

A CALLED GAME is one in which, for any reason, the umpire-in-chief terminates play.

A CATCH is the act of a fielder in getting secure possession in his hand or glove of a ball in flight and firmly holding it; providing he does not use his cap, protector, pocket or any other part of his uniform in getting possession. It is not a catch, however, if simultaneously or immediately following his contact with the ball, he collides with a player, or with a wall, or if he falls down, and as a result of such collision or falling, drops the ball. It is not a catch if a fielder touches a fly ball which then hits a member of the offensive team or an umpire and then is caught by another defensive player. If the fielder has made the catch and drops the ball while in the act of making a throw following the catch, the ball shall be adjudged to have been caught. In establishing the validity of the catch, the fielder shall hold the ball long enough to prove that he has complete control of the ball and that his release of the ball is voluntary and intentional.

A catch is legal if the ball is finally held by any fielder, even though juggled, or held by another fielder before it touches the ground. Runners may leave their bases the instant the first fielder touches the ball. A fielder may reach over a fence, railing, rope or other line of demarcation to make a catch. He may jump on top of a railing, or canvas that may be in foul ground. No interference should be allowed when a fielder reaches over a fence, railing, rope or into a stand to catch a ball. He does so at his own risk.

If a fielder, attempting a catch at the edge of the dugout, is "held up" and kept from an apparent fall by a player or players of either team and the catch is made, it shall be allowed.

The CATCHER is the fielder who takes his position back of the home base.

The CATCHER'S BOX is that area within which the catcher shall stand until the pitcher delivers the ball.

THE CLUB is a person or group of persons responsible for assembling the team personnel, providing the playing field and required facilities, and representing the team in relations with the league.

A COACH is a team member in uniform appointed by the manager to perform such duties as the manager may designate, such as but not limited to acting as base coach.

A DEAD BALL is a ball out of play because of a legally created temporary suspension of play.

The DEFENSE (or DEFENSIVE) is the team, or any player of the team, in the field.

A DOUBLE-HEADER is two regularly scheduled or rescheduled games, played in immediate succession.

A DOUBLE PLAY is a play by the defense in which two offensive players are put out as a result of continuous action, providing there is no error between putouts.

    (a) A force double play is one in which both putouts are force plays.

    (b) A reverse force double play is one in which the first out is a force play and the second out is made on a runner for whom the force is removed by reason of the first out. Examples of reverse force plays: runner on first, one out; batter grounds to first baseman, who steps on first base (one out) and throws to second baseman or shortstop for the second out (a tag play).

Another example: bases loaded, none out; batter grounds to third baseman, who steps on third base (one out), then throws to catcher for the second out (tag play).

DUGOUT (See definition of BENCH)

A FAIR BALL is a batted ball that settles on fair ground between home and first base, or between home and third base, or that is on or over fair territory when bounding to the outfield past first or third base, or that touches first, second or third base, or that first falls on fair territory on or beyond first base or third base, or that, while on or over fair territory, touches the person of an umpire or player, or that, while over fair territory, passes out of the playing field in flight.

A fair fly shall be judged according to the relative position of the ball and the foul line, including the foul pole, and not as to whether the fielder is on fair or foul territory at the time he touches the ball.

If a fly ball lands in the infield between home and first base, or home and third base, and then bounces to foul territory without touching a player or umpire and before passing first or third base, it is a foul ball; or if the ball settles on foul territory or is touched by a player on foul territory, it is a foul ball. If a fly ball lands on or beyond first or third base and then bounces to foul territory, it is a fair hit.

Clubs, increasingly, are erecting tall foul poles at the fence line with a wire netting extending along the side of the pole on fair territory above the fence to enable the umpires more accurately to judge fair and foul balls.

FAIR TERRITORY is that part of the playing field within, and including the first base and third base lines, from home base to the bottom of the playing field fence and perpendicularly upwards. All foul lines are in fair territory.

A FIELDER is any defensive player.

FIELDER'S CHOICE is the act of a fielder who handles a fair grounder and, instead of throwing to first base to put out the batter-runner, throws to another base in an attempt to put out a preceding runner. The term is also used by scorers (a) to account for the advance of the batter-runner who takes one or more extra bases when the fielder who handles his safe hit attempts to put out a preceding runner; (b) to account for the advance of a runner (other than by stolen base or error) while a fielder is attempting to put out another runner; and (c) to account for the advance of a runner solely because of the defensive team's indifference (undefended steal).

A FLY BALL is a batted ball that goes high in the air in flight.

A FORCE PLAY is a play in which a runner legally loses his right to occupy a base by reason of the batter becoming a runner.

Confusion regarding this play is removed by remembering that frequently the "force" situation is removed during the play. Example: Man on first, one out, ball hit sharply to first baseman who touches the bag and batter-runner is out. The force is removed at that moment and runner advancing to second must be tagged. If there had been a runner on third or second, and either of these runners scored before the tag-out at second, the run counts. Had the first baseman thrown to second and the ball then had been returned to first, the play at second was a force out, making two outs, and the return throw to first ahead of the runner would have made three outs. In that case, no run would score.

Example: Not a force out. One out. Runner on first and third. Batter flies out. Two out. Runner on third tags up and scores. Runner on first tries to retouch before throw from third baseman reaches first baseman, but does not get back in time and is out. Three outs. If, in umpire's judgment, the runner from third touched home before the ball was held at first base, the run counts.

A FORFEITED GAME is a game declared ended by the umpire-in-chief in favor of the offended team by the score of 9 to 0, for violation of the rules.

A FOUL BALL is a batted ball that settles on foul territory between home and first base, or between home and third base, or that bounds past first or third base on or over foul territory, or that first falls on foul territory beyond first or third base, or that, while on or over foul territory, touches the person of an umpire or player, or any object foreign to the natural ground.

A foul fly shall be judged according to the relative position of the ball and the foul line, including the foul pole, and not as to whether the fielder is on foul or fair territory at the time he touches the ball.

A batted ball not touched by a fielder, which hits the pitcher's rubber and rebounds into foul territory, between home and first, or between home and third base is a foul ball.

FOUL TERRITORY is that part of the playing field outside the first and third base lines extended to the fence and perpendicularly upwards.

A FOUL TIP is a batted ball that goes sharp and direct from the bat to the catcher's hands and is legally caught. It is not a foul tip unless caught and any foul tip that is caught is a strike, and the ball is in play. It is not a catch if it is a rebound, unless the ball has first touched the catcher's glove or hand.

A GROUND BALL is a batted ball that rolls or bounces close to the ground.

The HOME TEAM is the team on whose grounds the game is played, or if the game is played on neutral grounds, the home team shall be designated by mutual agreement.

ILLEGAL (or ILLEGALLY) is contrary to these rules.

An ILLEGAL PITCH is (1) a pitch delivered to the batter when the pitcher does not have his pivot foot in contact with the pitcher's plate; (2) a quick return pitch. An illegal pitch when runners are on base is a balk.

An INFIELDER is a fielder who occupies a position in the infield.

An INFIELD FLY is a fair fly ball (not including a line drive nor an attempted bunt) which can be caught by an infielder with ordinary effort, when first and second, or first, second and third bases are occupied, before two are out. The pitcher, catcher and any outfielder who stations himself in the infield on the play shall be considered infielders for the purpose of this rule.

When it seems apparent that a batted ball will be an Infield Fly, the umpire shall immediately declare "Infield Fly" for the benefit of the runners. If the ball is near the baselines, the umpire shall declare "Infield Fly, if Fair."

The ball is alive and runners may advance at the risk of the ball being caught, or retouch and advance after the ball is touched, the same as on any fly ball. If the hit becomes a foul ball, it is treated the same as any foul.

If a declared Infield Fly is allowed to fall untouched to the ground, and bounces foul before passing first or third base, it is a foul ball. If a declared Infield Fly falls untouched to the ground outside the baseline, and bounces fair before passing first or third base, it is an Infield Fly.

On the infield fly rule the umpire is to rule whether the ball could ordinarily have been handled by an infielder—not by some arbitrary limitation such as the grass, or the base lines. The umpire must also that a ball is an infield fly, even if handled by an outfielder, if, in the umpire's judgment, the ball could have been as easily handled by an infielder. The infield fly is in no sense to be considered an appeal play. The umpire's judgment must govern, and the decision should be made immediately.

When an infield fly rule is called, runners may advance at their own risk. If on an infield fly rule, the infielder intentionally drops a fair ball, the ball remains in play despite the provisions of Rule 6.05 (L). The infield fly rule takes precedence.

IN FLIGHT describes a batted, thrown, or pitched ball which has not yet touched the ground or some object other than a fielder.

IN JEOPARDY is a term indicating that the ball is in play and an offensive player may be put out.

An INNING is that portion of a game within which the teams alternate on offense and defense and in which there are three putouts for each team. Each team's time at bat is a half-inning.

INTERFERENCE

(a) Offensive interference is an act by the team at bat which interferes with, obstructs, impedes, hinders or confuses any fielder attempting to make a play. If the umpire declares the batter, batter-runner, or a runner out for interference, all other runners shall return to the last base that was, in the judgment of the umpire, legally touched at the time of the interference, unless otherwise provided by these rules.

In the event the batter-runner has not reached first base, all runners shall return to the base last occupied at the time of the pitch.

(b) Defensive interference is an act by a fielder which hinders or prevents a batter from hitting a pitch.

(c) Umpire's interference occurs (1) When an umpire hinders, impedes or prevents a catcher's throw attempting to prevent a stolen base, or (2) When a fair ball touches an umpire on fair territory before passing a fielder.

(d) Spectator interference occurs when a spectator reaches out of the stands, or goes on the playing field, and touches a live ball.

On any interference the ball is dead.

THE LEAGUE is a group of clubs whose teams play each other in a pre-arranged schedule under these rules for the league championship.

THE LEAGUE PRESIDENT shall enforce the official rules, resolve any disputes involving the rules, and determine any protested games. The league president may fine any player, coach, manager or umpire for violation of these rules, at his discretion.

LEGAL (or LEGALLY) is in accordance with these rules.

A LIVE BALL is a ball which is in play.

A LINE DRIVE is a batted ball that goes sharp and direct from the bat to a fielder without touching the ground.

THE MANAGER is a person appointed by the club to be responsible for the team's actions on the field, and to represent the team in communications with the umpire and the opposing team. A player may be appointed manager.

(a) The club shall designate the manager to the league president or the umpire-in-chief not less than thirty minutes before the scheduled starting time of the game.

(b) The manager may advise the umpire that he has delegated specific duties prescribed by the rules to a player or coach, and any action of such designated representative shall be official. The manager shall always be responsible for his team's conduct, observance of the official rules, and deference to the umpires.

(c) If a manager leaves the field, he shall designate a player or coach as his substitute, and such substitute manager shall have the duties, rights and responsibilities of the manager. If the manager fails or refuses to designate his substitute before leaving, the umpire-in-chief shall designate a team member as substitute manager.

OBSTRUCTION is the act of a fielder who, while not in possession of the ball and not in the act of fielding the ball, impedes the progress of any runner.

If a fielder is about to receive a thrown ball and if the ball is in flight directly toward and near enough to the fielder so he must occupy his position to receive the ball he may be considered "in the act of fielding a ball." It is entirely up to the judgment of the umpire as to whether a fielder is in the act of fielding a ball. After a fielder has made an attempt to field a ball and missed, he can no longer be in the "act of fielding" the ball. For example: an infielder dives at a ground ball and the ball passes him and he continues to lie on the ground and delays the progress of the runner, he very likely has obstructed the runner.

OFFENSE is the team, or any player of the team, at bat.

An OUT is one of the three required retirements of an offensive team during its time at bat.

An OUTFIELDER is a fielder who occupies a position in the outfield, which is the area of the playing field most distant from home base.

OVERSLIDE (or OVERSLIDING) is the act of an offensive player when his slide to a base, other than when advancing from home to first base, is with such momentum that he loses contact with the base.

A PENALTY is the application of these rules following an illegal act.

The PERSON of a player or an umpire is any part of his body, his clothing or his equipment.

A PITCH is a ball delivered to the batter by the pitcher.

All other deliveries of the ball by one player to another are thrown balls.

A PITCHER is the fielder designated to deliver the pitch to the batter.

The pitcher's PIVOT FOOT is that foot which is in contact with the pitcher's plate as he delivers the pitch.

"PLAY" is the umpire's order to start the game or to resume action following any dead ball.

A QUICK RETURN pitch is one made with obvious intent to catch a batter off balance. It is an illegal pitch.

REGULATION GAME. See Rules 4.10 and 4.11.

A RETOUCH is the act of a runner in returning to a base as legally required.

A RUN (or SCORE) is the score made by an offensive player who advances from batter to runner and touches first, second, third and home bases in that order.

A RUN-DOWN is the act of the defense in an attempt to put out a runner between bases.

A RUNNER is an offensive player who is advancing toward, or touching, or returning to any base.

"SAFE" is a declaration by the umpire that a runner is entitled to the base for which he was trying.

SET POSITION is one of the two legal pitching positions.

SQUEEZE PLAY is a term to designate a play when a team, with a runner on third base, attempts to score that runner by means of a bunt.

A STRIKE is a legal pitch when so called by the umpire, which—

(a) Is struck at by the batter and is missed;

(b) Is not struck at, if any part of the ball passes through any part of the strike zone;

(c) Is fouled by the batter when he has less than two strikes;

(d) Is bunted foul;

(e) Touches the batter as he strikes at it;

(f) Touches the batter in flight in the strike zone; or

(g) Becomes a foul tip.

The STRIKE ZONE is that space over home plate which is between the batter's armpits and the top of his knees when he assumes his natural stance. The umpire shall determine the strike zone according to the batter's usual stance when he swings at a pitch.

A SUSPENDED GAME is a called game which is to be completed at a later date.

A TAG is the action of a fielder in touching a base with his body while holding the ball securely and firmly in his hand or glove; or touching a runner with the ball, or with his hand or glove holding the ball, while holding the ball securely and firmly in his hand or glove.

A THROW is the act of propelling the ball with the hand and arm to a given objective and is to be distinguished, always, from the pitch.

A TIE GAME is a regulation game which is called when each team has the same number of runs.

"TIME" is the announcement by an umpire of a legal interruption of play, during which the ball is dead.

TOUCH. To touch a player or umpire is to touch any part of his body, his clothing or his equipment.

A TRIPLE PLAY is a play by the defense in which three offensive players are put out as a result of continuous action, providing there is no error between putouts.

A WILD PITCH is one so high, so low, or so wide of the plate that it cannot be handled with ordinary effort by the catcher.

WIND-UP POSITION is one of the two legal pitching positions.

3.00—Game Preliminaries.

3.01 Before the game begins the umpire shall—

(a) Require strict observance of all rules governing implements of play and equipment of players;

(b) Be sure that all playing lines are marked with lime, chalk or other white material easily distinguishable from the ground or grass;

(c) Receive from the home club a supply of regulation baseballs, the number and make to be certified to the home club by the league president. Each ball shall be enclosed in a sealed package bearing the signature of the league president, and the seal shall not be broken until just prior to game time when the umpire shall open each package to inspect the ball and remove its gloss. The umpire shall be the sole judge of the fitness of the balls to be used in the game;

(d) Be assured by the home club that at least one dozen regulation reserve balls are immediately available for use if required;

(e) Have in his possession at least two alternate balls and shall require replenishment of such supply of alternate balls as needed throughout the game. Such alternate balls shall be put in play when—

    (1) A ball has been batted out of the playing field or into the spectator area;

    (2) A ball has become discolored or unfit for futher use;

    (3) The pitcher requests such alternate ball.

The umpire shall not give an alternate ball to the pitcher until play has ended and the previously used ball is dead. After a thrown or batted ball goes out of the playing field, play shall not be resumed with an alternate ball until the runners have reached the bases to which they are entitled. After a home run is hit out of the playing grounds, the umpire shall not deliver a new ball to the pitcher or the catcher until the batter hitting the home run has crossed the plate.

3.02 No player shall intentionally discolor or damage the ball by rubbing it with soil, rosin, paraffin, licorice, sand-paper, emery-paper or other foreign substance.

    PENALTY: The umpire shall demand the ball and remove the offender from the game. In case the umpire cannot locate the offender, and if the pitcher delivers such discolored or damaged ball to the batter, the pitcher shall be removed from the game at once and shall be suspended automatically for ten days.

3.03 A player, or players, may be substituted during a game at any time the ball is dead. A substitute player shall bat in the replaced player's position in the team's batting order. A player once removed from a game shall not re-enter that game. If a substitute enters the game in place of a player-manager, the manager may thereafter go to the coaching lines at his discretion. When two or more substitute players of the defensive team enter the game at the same time, the manager shall, immediately before they take their positions as fielders, designate to the umpire-in-chief such players' positions in the team's batting order and the umpire-in-chief shall so notify the official scorer. If this information is not immediately given to the umpire-in-chief, he shall have authority to designate the substitutes' places in the batting order.

A pitcher may change to another position only once during the same inning; e.g. the pitcher will not be allowed to assume a position other than a pitcher more than once in the same inning.

Any player other than a pitcher substituted for an injured player shall be allowed five warm-up throws. (See Rule 8.03 for pitchers.)

3.04 A player whose name is on his team's batting order may not become a substitute runner for another member of his team.

This rule is intended to eliminate the practice of using so-called courtesy runners. No player in the game shall be permitted to act as a courtesy runner for a teammate. No player who has been in the game and has been taken out for a substitute shall return as a courtesy runner. Any player not in the line-up, if used as a runner, shall be considered as a substitute player.

3.05 (a) The pitcher named in the batting order handed the umpire-in-chief, as provided in Rules 4.01 (a) and 4.01 (b), shall pitch to the first batter or any substitute batter until such batter is put out or reaches first base, unless the pitcher sustains injury or illness which, in the judgment of the umpire-in-chief, incapacitates him from pitching.

    (b) If the pitcher is replaced, the substitute pitcher shall pitch to the batter then at bat, or any substitute batter, until such batter is put out or reaches first base, or until the offensive team is put out, unless the substitute pitcher sustains injury or illness which, in the umpire-in-chief's judgment, incapacitates him for further play as a pitcher.

    (c) **If an improper substitution is made for the pitcher, the umpire shall direct the proper pitcher to return to the game until the provisions of this rule are fulfilled. If the improper pitcher is permitted to pitch, any play that results is legal. The improper pitcher becomes the proper pitcher as soon as he makes his first pitch to the batter, or as soon as any runner is put out.**

If a manager attempts to remove a pitcher in violation of Rule 3.05 (c) the umpire shall notify the manager of the offending club that it cannot be done. If, by chance, the umpire-in-chief has, through oversight, announced the incoming improper pitcher, he should still correct the situation before the improper pitcher pitches. Once the improper pitcher delivers a pitch he becomes the proper pitcher.

3.06 The manager shall immediately notify the umpire-in-chief of any substitution and shall state to the umpire-in-chief the substitute's place in his batting order.

Players for whom substitutions have been made may remain with their team on the bench or may "warm-up" pitchers. If a manager substitutes another player for himself, he may continue to direct his team from the bench or the coach's box. Umpires should not permit players for whom substitutes have been made, and who are permitted to remain on the bench, to address any remarks to any opposing player or manager, or to the umpires.

3.07 The umpire-in-chief, after having been notified, shall immediately announce, or cause to be announced, each substitution.

3.08 (a) If no announcement of a substitution is made, the substitute shall be considered as having entered the game when—

    (1) If a pitcher, he takes his place on the pitcher's plate;

    (2) If a batter, he takes his place in the batter's box;

    (3) If a fielder, he reaches the position usually occupied by the fielder he has replaced, and play commences;

    (4) If a runner, he takes the place of the runner he has replaced.

    (b) Any play made by, or on, any of the above mentioned unannounced substitutes shall be legal.

3.09 Players in uniform shall not address or mingle with spectators, nor sit in the stands before, during, or after a game. No manager, coach or player shall address any spectator before or during a game. Players of opposing teams shall not fraternize at any time while in uniform.

3.10 (a) The manager of the home team shall be the sole judge as to whether a game shall be started because of unsuitable weather conditions or the unfit condition of the playing field, except for the second game of a doubleheader. EXCEPTION: Any league may permanently authorize its president to suspend the application of this rule as to that league dur-

ing the closing weeks of its championship season in order to assure that the championship is decided each year on its merits. When the postponement of, and possible failure to play, a game in the final series of a championship season between any two teams might affect the final standing of any club in the league, the president, on appeal from any league club, may assume the authority granted the home team manager by this rule.

    (b) The umpire-in-chief of the first game shall be the sole judge as to whether the second game of a doubleheader shall not be started because of unsuitable weather conditions or the unfit condition of the playing field.

    (c) The umpire-in-chief shall be the sole judge as to whether and when play shall be suspended during a game because of unsuitable weather conditions or the unfit condition of the playing field; as to whether and when they play shall be resumed after such suspenion; and as to whether and when a game shall be terminated after such suspension. He shall not call the game until at least thirty minutes after he has suspended play. He may continue the suspension as long as he believes there is any chance to resume play.

The umpire-in-chief shall at all times try to complete a game. His authority to resume play following one or more suspensions of as much as thirty minutes each shall be absolute and he shall terminate a game only when there appears to be no possibility of completing it.

3.11 Between games of a doubleheader, or whenever a game is suspended because of the unfitness of the playing field, the umpire-in-chief shall have control of ground-keepers and assistants for the purpose of making the playing field fit for play.

    PENALTY: For violation, the umpire-in-chief may forfeit the game to the visiting team.

3.12 When the umpire suspends play he shall call "Time." At the umpire's call of "Play," the suspension is lifted and play resumes. Between the call of "Time" and the call of "Play" the ball is dead.

3.13 The manager of the home team shall present to the umpire-in-chief and the opposing manager any ground rules he thinks necessary covering the overflow of spectators upon the playing field, batted or thrown balls into such overflow, or any other contingencies. If these rules are acceptable to the opposing manager they shall be legal. If these rules are unacceptable to the opposing manager, the umpire-in-chief shall make and enforce any special ground rules he thinks are made necessary by ground conditions, which shall not conflict with the official playing rules.

3.14 Members of the offensive team shall carry all gloves and other equipment off the field and to the dugout while their team is at bat. No equipment shall be left lying on the field, either in fair or foul territory.

3.15 No person shall be allowed on the playing field during a game except players and coaches in uniform, managers, news photographers authorized by the home team, umpires, officers of the law in uniform and watchmen or other employees of the home club. In case of unintentional interference with play by any person herein authorized to be on the playing field (except members of the offensive team participating in the game, or a coach in the coach's box, or an umpire) the ball is alive and in play. If the interference is intentional, the ball shall be dead at the moment of the interference and the umpire shall impose such penalties as in his opinion will nullify the act of interference.

    NOTE: See Rule 7.11 for individuals excepted above, also see Rule 7.08 (b).

The question of intentional or unintentional interference shall be decided on the basis of the person's action. For example: a bat boy, ball attendant, policeman, etc., who tries to avoid being touched by a thrown or batted ball but still is touched by the ball would be involved in unintentional interference. If, however, he kicks the ball or picks it up or pushes it, that is considered intentional interference, regardless of what his thought may have been.

PLAY: Batter hits ball to shortstop, who fields ball but throws wild past first baseman. The offensive coach at first base, to avoid being hit by the ball, falls to the ground and the first baseman on his way to retrieve the wild thrown ball, runs into the coach; the batter-runner finally ends up on third base. The question is asked whether the umpire should call interference on the part of the coach. This would be up to the judgment of the umpire and if the umpire felt that the coach did all he could to avoid interfering with the play, no interference need be called. If it appeared to the umpire that the coach was obviously just making it appear he was trying not to interfere, the umpire should rule interference.

3.16 When there is spectator interference with any thrown or batted ball, the ball shall be dead at the moment of interference and the umpire shall impose such penalties as in his opinion will nullify the act of interference.

    APPROVED RULING: If spectator interference clearly prevents a fielder from catching a fly ball, the umpire shall declare the batter out.

There is a difference between a ball which has been thrown or batted into the stands, touching a spectator thereby being out of play even though it rebounds onto the field and a spectator going onto the field or reaching over, under or through a barrier and touching a ball in play or touching or otherwise interfering with a player. In the latter case it is clearly intentional and shall be dealt with as intentional interference as in Rule 3.15. Batter and runners shall be placed where in the umpire's judgment they would have been had the interference not occurred.

No interference shall be allowed when a fielder reaches over a fence, railing, rope or into a stand to catch a ball. He does so at his own risk. However, should a spectator reach out on the playing field side of such fence, railing or rope, and plainly prevent the fielder from catching the ball, then the batsman should be called out for the spectator's interference.

Example: Runner on third base, one out and a batter hits a fly ball deep to the outfield (fair or foul). Spectator clearly interferes with the outfielder attempting to catch the fly ball. Umpires calls the batter out for spectator interference. Ball is dead at the time of the call. Umpire decides that because of the distance the ball was hit, the runner on third base would have scored after the catch if the fielder had caught the ball which was interfered with, therefore, the runner is permitted to score. This might not be the case if such fly ball was interefered with a short distance from home plate.

3.17 Players and substitutes of both teams shall confine themselves to their team's benches unless actually participating in the play or preparing to enter the game, or coaching at first or third base. No one except players, substitutes, managers, coaches, trainers and bat boys shall occupy a bench during a game.

PENALTY: For violation the umpire may, after warning, remove the offender from the field.

Players on the disabled list are permitted to participate in pre-game activity and sit on the bench during a game but may not take part in any activity during the game such as warming up a pitcher, bench-jockeying, etc. Disabled players are not allowed to enter the playing surface at any time or for any purpose during the game.

3.18 The home team shall provide police protection sufficient to preserve order. If a person, or persons, enter the playing field during a game and interfere in any way with the play, the visiting team may refuse to play until the field is cleared.

PENALTY: If the field is not cleared in a reasonable length of time, which shall in no case be less than fifteen minutes after the visiting team's refusal to play, the umpire may forfeit the game to the visiting team.

4.00—Starting and Ending a Game.

4.01 Unless the home club shall have given previous notice that the game has been postponed or will be delayed in starting, the umpire, or umpires, shall enter the playing field five minutes before the hour set for the game to begin and proceed directly to home base where they shall be met by the managers of the opposing teams.

In sequence—

(a) First, the home manager shall give his batting order to the umpire-in-chief, in duplicate.

(b) Next, the visiting manager shall give his batting order to the umpire-in-chief, in duplicate.

(c) The umpire-in-chief shall make certain that the original and copies of the respective batting orders are identical, and then tender a copy of each batting order to the opposing manager. The copy retained by the umpire shall be the official batting order. The tender of the batting order by the umpire shall establish the batting orders. Thereafter, no substitutions shall be made by either manager, except as provided in these rules.

(d) As soon as the home team's batting order is handed to the umpire-in-chief the umpires are in charge of the playing field and from that moment they shall have sole authority to determine when a game shall be called, suspended or resumed on account of weather or the condition of the playing field.

Obvious errors in the batting order, which are noticed by the umpire-in-chief before he calls "Play" for the start of the game, should be called to the attention of the manager or captain of the team in error, so the correction can be made before the game starts. For example, if a manager has inadvertently listed only eight men in the batting order, or has listed two players with the same last name but without an identifying initial and the errors are noticed by the umpire before he calls "play," he shall cause such error or errors to be corrected before he calls "play" to start the game. Teams should not be "trapped" later by some mistake that obviously was inadvertent and which can be corrected before the game starts.

4.02 The players of the home team shall take their defensive positions, the first batter of the visiting team shall take his position in the batter's box, the umpire shall call "Play" and the game shall start.

4.03 When the ball is put in play at the start of, or during a game, all fielders other than the catcher shall be on fair territory.

(a) The catcher shall station himself directly back of the plate. He may leave his position at any time to catch a pitch or make a play except that when the batter is being given an intentional base on balls, the catcher must stand with both feet within the lines of the catcher's box until the ball leaves the pitcher's hand.

PENALTY: Balk.

(b) The pitcher, while in the act of delivering the ball to the batter, shall take his legal position;

(c) Except the pitcher and the catcher, any fielder may station himself anywhere in fair territory;

(d) Except the batter, or a runner attempting to score, no offensive player shall cross the catcher's lines when the ball is in play.

4.04 The batting order shall be followed throughout the game unless a player is substituted for another. In that case the substitute shall take the place of the replaced player in the batting order.

4.05 (a) The offensive team shall station two base coaches on the field during its term at bat, one near first base and one near third base.

(b) Base coaches shall be limited to two in number and shall (1) be in team uniform, and (2) remain within the coach's box at all times.

PENALTY: The offending base coach shall be removed from the game, and shall leave the playing field.

It has been common practice for many years for some coaches to put one foot outside the coach's box or stand astride or otherwise be slightly outside the coaching box lines. The coach shall not be considered out of the box unless the opposing manager complains, and then, the umpire shall strictly enforce the rule and require all coaches (on both teams) to remain in the coach's box at all times.

It is also common practice for a coach who has a play at his base to leave the coach's box to signal the player to slide, advance or return to a base. This may be allowed if the coach does not interfere with the play in any manner.

4.06 (a) No manager, player, substitute, coach, trainer or batboy shall at any time, whether from the bench, the coach's box or on the playing field, or elsewhere—

(1) Incite, or try to incite, by word or sign a demonstration by spectators;

(2) Use language which will in any manner refer to or reflect upon opposing players, an umpire, or any spectator;

(3) Call "Time," or employ any other word or phrase or commit any act while the ball is alive and in play for the obvious purpose of trying to make the pitcher commit a balk.

(4) Make intentional contact with the umpire in any manner.

(b) No fielder shall take a position in the batter's line of vision, and with deliberate unsportsmanlike intent, act in a manner to distract the batter.

PENALTY: The offender shall be removed from the game and shall leave the playing field, and, if a balk is made, it shall be nullified.

4.07 When a manager, player, coach or trainer is ejected from a game, he shall leave the field immediately and take no further part in that game. He shall remain in the club house or change to street clothes and either leave the park or take a seat in the grandstand well removed from the vicinity of his team's bench or bullpen.

If a manager, coach or player is under suspension he may not be in the dugout or press box during the course of a game.

4.08 When the occupants of a player's bench show violent disapproval of an umpire's decision, the umpire shall first give warning that such disapproval shall cease. If such action continues—

PENALTY: The umpire shall order the offenders from the bench to the club house. If he is unable to detect the offender, or offenders, he may clear the bench of all substitute players. The manager of the offending team shall have the privilege of recalling to the playing field only those players needed for substitution in the game.

4.09 HOW A TEAM SCORES.

(a) One run shall be scored each time a runner legally advances to and touches first, second, third and home base before three men are put out to end the inning. EXCEPTION: A run is not scored if the runner advances to home base during a play in which the third out is made (1) by the batter-runner before he touches first base; (2) by any runner being forced out; or (3) by a preceding runner who is declared out because he failed to touch one of the bases.

(b) When the winning run is scored in the last half-inning of a regulation game, or in the last half of an extra inning, as the result of a base on balls, hit batter or any other play with the bases full which forces the runner on third to advance, the umpire shall not declare the game ended until the runner forced to advance from third has touched home base and the batter-runner has touched first base.

An exception will be if fans rush onto the field and physically prevent the runner from touching home plate or the batter from touching first base. In such cases, the umpires shall award the runner the base because of the obstruction by the fans.

PENALTY: If the runner on third refuses to advance to and touch home base in a reasonable time, the umpire shall disallow the run and order the offending player and order the game resumed. If, with two out, the batter-runner refuses to advance to and touch first base, the umpire shall disallow the run, call out the offending player, and order the game resumed. If, before two are out, the batter-runner refuses to advance to and touch first base, the run shall count, but the offending player shall be called out.

Approved Ruling: No run shall score during a play in which the third out is made by the batter-runner before he touches first base. Example: One out, Jones on second, Smith on first. The batter, Brown, hits safely. Jones scores. Smith is out on the throw to plate. Two outs. But Brown missed first base. The ball is thrown to first, an appeal is made, and Brown is out. Three outs. Since Brown crossed the plate during a play in which the third out was made by the batter-runner before he touched first base, Jones' run does not count.

Approved Ruling: Following runners are not affected by an act of a preceding runner unless two are out.

Example: One out, Jones on second, Smith on first, and batter, Brown, hits home run inside the park. Jones fails to touch third on his way to the plate. Smith and Brown score. The defense holds the ball on third, appeals to umpire, and Jones is out. Smith's and Brown's runs count.

Approved Ruling: Two out, Jones on second, Smith on first and batter, Brown, hits home run inside the park. All three runs cross the plate. But Jones missed third base, and on appeal is declared out. Three outs. Smith's and Brown's runs are voided. No score on the play.

Approved Ruling: One out, Jones on third, Smith on second. Batter Brown flies out to center. Two out. Jones scores after catch and Smith scores on bad throw to plate. But Jones, on appeal, is adjudged to have left third before the catch and is out. Three outs. No runs.

Approved Ruling: Two out, bases full, batter hits home run over fence. Batter, on appeal, is declared out for missing first base. Three outs. No run counts.

Here is a general statement that covers:

When a runner misses a base and a fielder holds the ball on a missed base, or on the base originally occupied by the runner if a fly ball is caught, and appeals for the umpire's decision, the runner is out when the umpire sustains the appeal; all runners may score if possible, except that with two out the runner is out at the moment he misses the bag, if an appeal is sustained as applied to the following runners.

Approved Ruling: One out, Jones on third, Smith on first, and Brown flies out to right field. Two outs. Jones tags up and scores after the catch. Smith attempted to return to first but the right fielder's throw beat him to the base. Three outs. But Jones scored before the throw to catch Smith reached first base, hence Jones' run counts. It was not a force play.

4.10 (a) A regulation game consists of nine innings, unless extended because of a tie score, or shortened (1) because the home team needs none of its half of the ninth inning or only a fraction of it, or (2) because the umpire calls the game. EXCEPTION: National Association leagues may adopt a rule providing that one or both games of a doubleheader shall be seven innings in length. In such games, any of these rules applying to the ninth inning shall apply to the seventh inning.

(b) If the score is tied after nine completed innings play shall continue until (1) the visiting team has scored more total runs than the home team at the end of a completed inning, or (2) the home team scores the winning run in an uncompleted inning.

(c) If a game is called, it is a regulation game:
(1) If five innings have been completed;
(2) If the home team has scored more runs in four or four and a fraction half-innings than the visiting team has scored in five completed half-innings;
(3) If the home team scores one or more runs in its half of the fifth inning to tie the score.

(d) If each team has the same number of runs when the game ends, the umpire shall declare it a "Tie Game."

(e) If a game is called before it has become a regulation game, the umpire shall declare it "No Game."

(f) Rain checks will not be honored for any regulation or suspended game which has progressed to or beyond a point of play described in 4.10(c).

4.11 The score of a regulation game is the total number of runs scored by each team at the moment the game ends.

(a) The game ends when the visiting team completes its half of the ninth inning if the home team is ahead.

(b) The game ends when the ninth inning is completed, if the visiting team is ahead.

(c) If the home team scores the winning run in its half of the ninth inning (or its half of an extra inning after a tie) the game ends immediately when the winning run is scored. EXCEPTION: If the last batter in a game hits a home run out of the playing field, the batter-runner and all runners on base are permitted to score, in accordance with the base-running rules, and the game ends when the batter-runner touches home plate.

APPROVED RULING: The batter hits a home run out of the playing field to win the game in the last half of the ninth or an extra inning, but is called out for passing a preceding runner. The game ends immediately when the winning run is scored.

(d) A called game ends at the moment the umpire terminates play. EXCEPTION: If the game is called while an inning is in progress and before it is completed, the game becomes a SUSPENDED game in each of the following situations:

(1) The visiting team has scored one or more runs to tie the score and the home team has not scored;

(2) The visiting team has scored one or more runs to take the lead and the home team has not tied the score or retaken the lead.

National Association Leagues may also adopt the following rules for suspended games in addition to 4.11 (d) (1) & (2) above. (If adopted by a National Association League, Rule 4.10 (c) (d) & (e) would not apply to their games.):

(3) The game has not become a regulation game (4½ innings with the home team ahead, or 5 innings with the visiting club ahead or tied).

(4) Any regulation game tied at the point play is stopped because of weather, curfew or other reason.

(5) If a game is suspended before it becomes a regulation game, and is continued prior to another regularly scheduled game, the regularly scheduled game will be limited to seven innings.

(6) If a game is suspended after it is a regulation game, and is continued prior to another regularly scheduled game, the regularly scheduled game will be a nine inning game.

EXCEPTION: The above sections (3), (4), (5) & (6) will not apply to the last scheduled game between the two teams during the championship season, or League Playoffs.

Any suspended game not completed prior to the last scheduled game between the two teams during the championship season, will become a called game.

4.12 SUSPENDED GAMES.

(a) A league shall adopt the following rules providing for completion at a future date of games terminated for any of the following reasons:

(1) A curfew imposed by law;

(2) A time limit permissible under league rules;

(3) Light failure or malfunction of a mechanical field device under control of the home club. (Mechanical field device shall include automatic tarpaulin or water removal equipment).

(4) Darkness, when a law prevents the lights from being turned on.

(5) Weather, if the game is called while an inning is in progress and before it is completed, and one of the following situations prevails:

(i) The visiting team has scored one or more runs to tie the score, and the home team has not scored.

(ii) The visiting team has scored one or more runs to take the lead, and the home team has not tied the score or retaken the lead.

(b) Such games shall be known as suspended games. No game called because of a curfew, weather, or a time limit shall be a suspended game unless it has progressed far enough to have been a regulation game under the provisions of Rule 4.10. A game called under the provisions of 4.12(a), (3) or (4) shall be a suspended game at any time after it starts.

NOTE: Weather and similar conditions—4.12 (a) (1 through 5)—shall take precedence in determining whether a called game shall be a suspended game. A game can only be considered a suspended game if stopped for any of the five (5) reasons specified in Section (a). Any legal game called due to weather with the score tied (unless situation outlined in 4.12 (a) (5) (i) prevails) is a tie game and must be replayed in its entirety.

(c) A suspended game shall be resumed and completed as follows:

(1) Immediately preceding the next scheduled single game between the two clubs on the same grounds; or

(2) Immediately preceding the next scheduled doubleheader between the two clubs on the same grounds, if no single game remains on the schedule; or

(3) If suspended on the last scheduled date between the two clubs in that city, transferred and played on the grounds of the opposing club, if possible;

(i) Immediately preceding the next scheduled single game, or

(ii) Immediately preceding the next scheduled doubleheader, if no single game remains on the schedule.

(4) If a suspended game has not been resumed and completed on the last date scheduled for the two clubs, it shall be a called game.

(d) A suspended game shall be resumed at the exact point of suspension of the original game. The completion of a suspended game is a continuation of the original game. The lineup and batting order of both teams shall be exactly the same as the lineup and batting order at the moment of suspension, subject to the rules governing substitution. Any player may be replaced by a player who had not been in the game prior to the suspension. No player removed before the suspension may be returned to the lineup.

A player who was not with the club when the game was suspended may be used as a substitute, even if he has taken the place of a player no longer with the club who would not have been eligible because he had been removed from the lineup before the game was suspended.

If immediately prior to the call of a suspended game, a substitute pitcher has been announced but has not retired the side or pitched until the batter becomes a baserunner, such pitcher, when the suspended game is later resumed may, but is not required to start the resumed portion of the game. However, if he does not start he will be considered as having been substituted for and may not be used in that game.

(e) Rain checks will not be honored for any regulation or suspended game which has progressed to or beyond a point of play described in 4.10 (c).

4.13 RULES GOVERNING DOUBLEHEADERS.

(a) (1) Only two championship games shall be played on one date. Completion of a suspended game shall not violate this rule.

(2) If two games are scheduled to be played for one admission on one date, the first game shall be the regularly scheduled game for that date.

(b) After the start of the first game of a doubleheader, that game shall be completed before the second game of the doubleheader shall begin.

(c) The second game of a doubleheader shall start twenty minutes after the first game is completed, unless a longer interval (not to exceed thirty minutes) is declared by the umpire-in-chief and announced to the opposing managers at the end of the first game. EXCEPTION: If the league president has approved a request of the home club for a longer interval between games for some special event, the umpire-in-chief shall declare such longer interval and announced it to the opposing managers. The umpire-in-chief of the first game shall be the timekeeper controlling the interval between games.

(d) The umpire shall start the second game of a doubleheader, if at all possible, and play shall continue as long as ground conditions, local time restrictions, or weather permit.

(e) When a regularly scheduled doubleheader is delayed in starting for any cause, any game that is started is the first game of the doubleheader.

(f) When a rescheduled game is part of a doubleheader the rescheduled game shall be the second game, and the first game shall be the regularly scheduled game for that date.

4.14 The umpire-in-chief shall order the playing field lights turned on whenever in his opinion darkness makes further play in daylight hazardous.

4.15 A game may be forfeited to the opposing team when a team—

(a) Fails to appear upon the field, or being upon the field, refuses to start play within five minutes after the umpire has called "Play" at the appointed hour for beginning the game, unless such delayed appearance is, in the umpire's judgment, unavoidable;

(b) Employs tactics palpably designed to delay or shorten the game;

(c) Refuses to continue play during a game unless the game has been suspended or terminated by the umpire;

(d) Fails to resume play, after a suspension, within one minute after the umpire has called "Play;"

(e) After warning by the umpire, wilfully and persistently violates any rules of the game;

(f) Fails to obey within a reasonable time the umpire's order for removal of a player from the game;

(g) Fails to appear for the second game of a doubleheader within twenty minutes after the close of the first game unless the umpire-in-chief of the first game shall have extended the time of the intermission.

4.16 A game shall be forfeited to the visiting team if, after it has been suspended, the order of the umpire to groundskeepers respecting preparation of the field for resumption of play are not complied with.

4.17 A game shall be forfeited to the opposing team when a team is unable or refuses to place nine players on the field.

4.18 If the umpire declares a game forfeited he shall transmit a written report to the league president within twenty-four hours thereafter, but failure of such transmittal shall not effect the forfeiture.

4.19 PROTESTING GAMES. Each league shall adopt rules governing procedure for protesting a game, when a manager claims that an umpire's decision is in violation of these rules. No protest shall ever be permitted on judgment decisions by the umpire. In all protested games, the decision of the League President shall be final.

Even if it is held that the protested decision violated the rules, no replay of the game will be ordered unless in the opinion of the League President the violation adversely affected the protesting team's chances of winning the game.

Whenever a manager protests a game because of alleged misapplication of the rules the protest will not be recognized unless the umpires are notified at the time the play under protest occurs and before the next pitch is made or a runner is retired. A protest arising on a game-ending play may be filed until 12 noon the following day with the League Office.

5.00—Putting the Ball in Play. Live Ball

5.01 At the time set for beginning the game the umpire shall call "Play."

5.02 After the umpire calls "Play" the ball is alive and in play and remains alive and in play until for legal cause, or at the umpire's call of "Time" suspending play, the ball becomes dead. While the ball is dead no player may be put out, no bases may be run and no runs may be scored, except that runners may advance one or more bases as the result of acts which occurred while the ball was alive (such as, but not limited to balk, an overthrow, interference, or a home run or other fair hit out of the playing field).

Should a ball come partially apart in a game, it is in play until the play is completed.

5.03 The pitcher shall deliver the pitch to the batter who may elect to strike the ball, or who may not offer at it, as he chooses.

5.04 The offensive team's objective is to have its batter become a runner, and its runners advance.

5.05 The defensive team's objective is to prevent offensive players from becoming runners, and to prevent their advance around the bases.

5.06 When a batter becomes a runner and touches all bases legally he shall score one run for his team.

A run legally scored cannot be nullified by subsequent action of the runner, such as but not limited to an effort to return to third base in the belief that he had left the base before a caught fly ball.

5.07 When three offensive players are legally put out, that team takes the field and the opposing team becomes the offensive team.

5.08 If a thrown ball accidently touches a base coach, or a pitched or thrown ball touches an umpire, the ball is alive and in play. However, if the coach interferes with a thrown ball, the runner is out.

5.09 The ball becomes dead and runners advance one base, or return to their bases, without liability to be put out, when—

    (a) A pitched ball touches a batter, or his clothing, while in his legal batting position; runners, if forced, advance;

    (b) The plate umpire interferes with the catcher's throw; runners may not advance.

        NOTE: The interference shall be disregarded if the catcher's throw retires the runner.

    (c) A balk is committed; runners advance; (See Penalty 8.05)
    (d) A ball is illegally batted; runners return;
    (e) A foul ball is not caught; runners return. The umpire shall not put the ball in play until all runners have retouched their bases;
    (f) A fair ball touches a runner or an umpire on fair territory before it touches an infielder including the pitcher, or touches an umpire before it has passed an infielder other than the pitcher;

If a fair ball touches an umpire working in the infield after it has bounded past, or over, the pitcher, it is a dead ball. If a batted ball is deflected by a fielder in fair territory and hits a runner or an umpire while still in flight and then caught by an infielder it shall not be a catch, but the ball shall remain in play.

If a fair ball goes through, or by, an infielder, and touches a runner immediately back of him, or touches a runner after being deflected by an infielder, the ball is in play and the umpire shall not declare the runner out. In making such decision the umpire must be convinced that the ball passed through, or by, the infielder and that no other infielder had the chance to make a play on the ball; runners advance, if forced;

    (g) A pitched ball lodges in the umpire's or catcher's mask or paraphernalia, and remains out of play, runners advance one base;

If a foul tip hits the umpire and is caught by a fielder on the rebound, the ball is "dead" and the batsman cannot be called out. The same shall apply where such foul tip lodges in the umpire's mask or other paraphernalia.

If a third strike (not a foul tip) passes the catcher and hits an umpire, the ball is in play. If such ball rebounds and is caught by a fielder before it touches the ground, the batsman is not out on such a catch, but the ball remains in play and the batsman may be retired at first base, or touched with the ball for the out.

If a pitched ball lodges in the umpire's or catcher's mask or paraphernalia, and remains out of play, on the third strike or fourth ball, then the batter is entitled to first base and all runners advance one base. If the count on the batter is less than three balls, runners advance one base.

    (h) Any legal pitch touches a runner trying to score; runners advance.

5.10 The ball becomes dead when an umpire calls "Time." The umpire-in-chief shall call "Time"—

    (a) When in his judgment weather, darkness or similiar conditions make immedate further play impossible;

    (b) When light failure makes it difficult or impossible for the umpires to follow the play;

        NOTE: A league may adopt its own regulations governing games interrupted by light failure.

    (c) When an accident incapacitates a player or an umpire;
        (1) If an accident to a runner is such as to prevent him from proceeding to a base to which he is entitled, as on a home run hit out of the playing field, or an award of one or more bases, a substitute runner shall be permitted to complete the play.

    (d) When a manager requests "Time" for a substitution, or for a conference with one of his players.

    (e) When the umpire wishes to examine the ball, to consult with either manager, or for any similar cause.

    (f) When a fielder, after catching a fly ball, falls into a bench or stand, or falls across ropes into a crowd when spectators are on

the field. As pertains to runners, the provisions of 7.04 (c) shall prevail.

If a fielder after making a catch steps into a bench, but does not fall, the ball is in play and runners may advance at their own peril.

    (g) When an umpire orders a player or any other person removed from the playing field.

    (h) Except in the cases stated in paragraphs (b) and (c) (1) of this rule, no umpire shall call "Time" while a play is in progress.

5.11 After the ball is dead, play shall be resumed when the pitcher taks his place on the pitcher's plate with a new ball or the same ball in his possession and the plate umpire calls "Play." The plate umpire shall call "Play" as soon as the pitcher takes his place on his plate with the ball in his possession.

6.00—The Batter

6.01 (a) Each player of the offensive team shall bat in the order that his name appears in his team's batting order.

    (b) The first batter in each inning after the first inning shall be the player whose name follows that of the last player who legally completed his time at bat in the preceding inning.

6.02 (a) The batter shall take his position in the batter's box promptly when it is his time at bat.

    (b) The batter shall not leave his position in the batter's box after the pitcher comes to Set Position, or starts his windup.

        PENALTY: If the pitcher pitches, the umpire shall call "Ball" or "Strike," as the case may be.

The batter leaves the batter's box at the risk of having a strike delivered and called, unless he requests the umpire to call "Time." The batter is not at liberty to step in and out of the batter's box at will.

Once a batter has taken his position in the batter's box, he shall not be permitted to step out of the batter's box in order to use the resin or the pine tar rag, unless there is a delay in the game action or, in the judgment of the umpires, weather conditions warrant an exception.

Umpires will not call "Time" at the request of the batter or any member of his team once the pitcher has started his windup or has come to a set position even though the batter claims "dust in his eyes," "steamed glasses," "didn't get the sign" or for any other cause.

Umpires may grant a hitter's request for "Time" once he is in the batter's box, but the umpire should eliminate hitters walking out of the batter's box without reason. If umpires are not lenient, batters will understand that they are in the batter's box and they must remain there until the ball is pitched.

If pitcher delays once the batter is in his box and the umpire feels that the delay is not justified he may allow the batter to step out of the box momentarily.

If after the pitcher starts his wind-up or comes to a "set position" with a runner on, he does not go through with his pitch because the batter has stepped out of the box, it shall not be called a balk. Both the pitcher and batter have violated a rule and the umpire shall call time and both the batter and pitcher start over from "scratch."

    (c) If the batter refuses to take his position in the batter's box during his time at bat, the umpire shall order the pitcher to pitch, and shall call "Strike" on each such pitch. The batter may take his proper position after any such pitch, and the regular ball and strike count shall continue, but if he does not take his proper position before three strikes are called, he shall be declared out.

6.03 The batter's legal position shall be with both feet within the batter's box.

    APPROVED RULING: The lines defining the box are within the batter's box.

6.04 A batter has legally completed his time at bat when he is put out or becomes a runner.

6.05 A batter is out when—

    (a) His fair or foul fly ball (other than a foul tip) is legally caught by a fielder;

    (b) A third strike is legally caught by the catcher;

"Legally caught" means in the catcher's glove before the ball touches the ground. It is not legal if the ball lodges in his clothing or paraphernalia; or if it touches the umpire and is caught by the catcher on the rebound.

If a foul-tip first strikes the catcher's glove and then goes on through and is caught by both hands against his body or protector, before the ball touches the ground, it is a strike, and if third strike, batter is out. If smothered against his body or protector, it is a catch provided the ball struck the catcher's glove or hand first.

    (c) A third strike is not caught by the catcher when first base is occupied before two are out;

    (d) He bunts foul on third strike;

    (e) An Infield Fly is declared;

    (f) He attempts to hit a third strike and the ball touches him;

    (g) His fair ball touches him before touching a fielder;

    (h) After hitting or bunting a fair ball, his bat hits the ball a second time in fair territory. The ball is dead and no runners may advance. If the batter-runner drops his bat and the ball rolls against the bat in fair territory and, in the umpire's judgment, there was no intention to interfere with the course of the ball, the ball is alive and in play;

If a bat breaks and part of it is in fair territory and is hit by a batted ball or part of it hits a runner or fielder, play shall continue and no interference called. If batted ball hits part of broken bat in foul territory, it is a foul ball.

If a whole bat is thrown into fair territory and interferes with a defensive player attempting to make a play, interference shall be called, whether intentional or not.

In cases where the batting helmet is accidentally hit with a batted or thrown ball, the ball remains in play the same as if it has not hit the helmet.

If a batted ball strikes a batting helmet or any other object foreign to the natural ground while on foul territory, it is a foul ball and the ball is dead.

If, in the umpire's judgment, there is intent on the part of a baserunner to interfere with a batted or thrown ball by dropping the helmet or throwing it at the ball, then the runner would be out, the ball dead and runners would return to last base legally touched.

    (i) After hitting or bunting a foul ball, he intentionally deflects the course of the ball in any manner while running to first base. The ball is dead and no runners may advance;

    (j) After a third strike or after he hits a fair ball, he or first base is tagged before he touches first base;

(k) In running the last half of the distance from home base to first base, while the ball is being fielded to first base, he runs outside (to the right of) the three-foot line, or inside (to the left of) the foul line, and in the umpire's judgment in so doing interferes with the fielder taking the throw at first base; except that he may run outside (to the right of) the three-foot line or inside (to the left of) the foul line to avoid a fielder attempting to field a batted ball;

(l) An infielder intentionally drops a fair fly ball or line drive, with first, first and second, first and third, or first, second and third base occupied before two are out. The ball is dead and runner or runners shall return to their original base or bases;

APPROVED RULING: In this situation, the batter is not out if the infielder permits the ball to drop untouched to the ground, except when the Infield Fly rule applies.

(m) A preceding runner shall, in the umpire's judgment, intentionally interfere with a fielder who is attempting to catch a thrown ball or to throw a ball in an attempt to complete any play;

The objective of this rule is to penalize the offensive team for deliberate, unwarranted, unsportsmanlike action by the runner in leaving the baseline for the obvious purpose of crashing the pivot man on a double play, rather than trying to reach the base. Obviously this is an umpire's judgment play.

(n) With two out, a runner on third base, and two strikes on the batter, the runner attempts to steal home base on a legal pitch and the ball touches the runner in the batter's strike zone. The umpire shall call "Strike Three," the batter is out and the run shall not count; before two are out, the umpire shall call "Strike Three," the ball is dead, and the run counts.

6.06 A batter is out for illegal action when—

(a) He hits a ball with one or both feet on the ground entirely outside the batter's box.

If a batter hits a ball fair or foul while out of the batter's box, he shall be called out. Umpires should pay particular attention to the position of the batter's feet if he attempts to hit the ball while he is being intentionally passed. A batter cannot jump or step out of the batter's box and hit the ball.

(b) He steps from one batter's box to the other while the pitcher is in position ready to pitch;

(c) He interferes with the catcher's fielding or throwing by stepping out of the batter's box or making any other movement that hinders the catcher's play at home base. EXCEPTION: Batter is not out if any runner attempting to advance is put out, or if runner trying to score is called out for batter's interference.

If the batter interferes with the catcher, the plate umpire shall call "interference." The batter is out and the ball dead. No player may advance on such interference (offensive interference) and all runners must return to the last base that was, in the judgment of the umpire, legally touched at the time of the interference.

If, however, the catcher makes a play and a runner attempting to advance is put out, it is to be assumed there was no actual interference and that runner is out—not the batter. Any other runners on the base at the time may advance as the ruling is that there is no actual interference if a runner is retired. In that case play proceeds just as if no violation had been called.

If a batter strikes at a ball and misses and swings so hard he carries the bat all the way around and, in the umpire's judgment, unintentionally hits the catcher or the ball in back of him on the backswing before the catcher has securely held the ball, it shall be called a strike only (not interference). The ball will be dead, however, and no runner shall advance on the play.

(d) He uses or attempts to use a bat that, in the umpire's judgment, has been altered or tampered with in such a way to improve the distance factor or cause an unusual reaction on the baseball. This includes, bats that are filled, flat-surfaced, nailed, hollowed, grooved or covered with a substance such as paraffin, wax, etc.

No advancement on the bases will be allowed and any out or outs made during a play shall stand.

In addition to being called out, the player shall be ejected from the game and may be subject to additional penalties as determined by his League President.

6.07 BATTING OUT OF TURN.

(a) A batter shall be called out, on appeal, when he fails to bat in his proper turn, and another batter completes a time at bat in his place.

(1) The proper batter may take his place in the batter's box at any time before the improper batter becomes a runner or is put out, and any balls and strikes shall be counted in the proper batter's time at bat.

(b) When an improper batter becomes a runner or is put out, and the defensive team appeals to the umpire before the first pitch to the next batter of either team, or before any play or attempted play, the umpire shall (1) declare the proper batter out; and (2) nullify any advance or score made because of a ball batted by the improper batter or because of the improper batter's advance to first base on a hit, an error, a base on balls, a hit batter or otherwise.

NOTE: If a runner advances, while the improper batter is at bat, on a stolen base, balk, wild pitch or passed ball, such advance is legal.

(c) When an improper batter becomes a runner or is put out, and a pitch is made to the next batter of either team before an appeal is made, the improper batter thereby becomes the proper batter, and the results of his time at bat become legal.

(d) (1) When the proper batter is called out because he has failed to bat in turn, the next batter shall be the batter whose name follows that of the proper batter thus called out; (2) When an improper batter becomes a proper batter because no appeal is made before the next pitch, the next batter shall be the batter whose name follows that of such legalized improper batter. The instant an improper batter's actions are legalized, the batting order picks up with the name following that of the legalized improper batter.

The umpire shall not direct the attention of any person to the presence in the batter's box of an improper batter. This rule is designed to require constant vigilance by the players and managers of both teams.

There are two fundamentals to keep in mind: When a player bats out of turn, the proper batter is the player called out. If an improper batter bats and reaches base or is out and no appeal is made before a pitch to the next batter, or before any play or attempted play, that improper batter is considered to have batted in proper turn and establishes the order that is to follow.

APPROVED RULING

To illustrate various situations arising from batting out of turn, assume a first-inning batting order as follows:

Abel - Baker - Charles - Daniel - Edward - Frank - George - Hooker - Irwin.

PLAY (1). Baker bats. With the count 2 balls and 1 strike, (a) the offensive team discovers the error or (b) the defensive team appeals. RULING: In either case, Abel replaces Baker, with the count on him 2 balls and 1 strike.

PLAY (2). Baker bats and doubles. The defensive team appeals (a) immediately or (b) after a pitch to Charles. RULING: (a) Abel is called out and Baker is the proper batter; (b) Baker stays on second and Charles is the proper batter.

PLAY (3). Abel walks. Baker walks. Charles forces Baker. Edward bats in Daniel's turn. While Edward is at bat, Abel scores and Charles goes to second on a wild pitch. Edward grounds out, sending Charles to third. The defensive team appeals (a) immediately or (b) after a pitch to Daniel. RULING: (a) Abel's run counts and Charles is entitled to second base since these advances were not made because of the improper batter batting a ball or advancing to first base. Charles must return to second base because his advance to third resulted from the improper batter batting a ball. Daniel is called out, and Edward is the proper batter; (b) Abel's run counts and Charles stays on third. The proper batter is Frank.

PLAY (4). With the bases full and two out. Hooker bats in Frank's turn, and triples, scoring three runs. The defensive team appeals (a) immediately, or (b) after a pitch to George. RULING: (a) Frank is called out and no runs score. George is the proper batter to lead off the second inning; (b) Hooker stays on third and three runs score. Irwin is the proper batter.

PLAY (5). After Play (4) (b) above, George continues at bat. (a) Hooker is picked off third base for the third out, or (b) George flies out, and no appeal is made. Who is the proper leadoff batter in the second inning? RULING: (a) Irwin. He became the proper batter as soon as the first pitch to George legalized Hooker's triple; (b) Hooker. When no appeal was made, the first pitch to the leadoff batter of the opposing team legalized George's time at bat.

PLAY (6). Daniel walks and Abel comes to bat. Daniel was an improper batter, and if an appeal is made before the first pitch to Abel, Abel is out, Daniel is removed from base, and Baker is the proper batter. There is no appeal, and a pitch is made to Abel. Daniel's walk is now legalized, and Edward thereby becomes the proper batter. Edward can replace Abel at any time before Abel is put out or becomes a runner. He does not do so. Abel flies out, and Baker comes to bat. Abel was an improper batter, and if an appeal is made before the first pitch to Baker, Edward is out, and the proper batter is Frank. There is no appeal, and a pitch is made to Baker. Abel's out is now legalized, and the proper batter is Baker. Baker walks. Charles is the proper batter. Charles flies out. Now Daniel is the proper batter, but he is on second base. Who is the proper batter? RULING: The proper batter is Edward. When the proper batter is on base, he is passed over, and the following batter becomes the proper batter.

6.08 The batter becomes a runner and is entitled to first base without liability to be put out (provided he advances to and touches first base) when—

(a) Four "balls" have been called by the umpire;

A batter who is entitled to first base because of a base on balls must go to first base and touch the base before other base runners are forced to advance. This applies when bases are full and applies when a substitute runner is put into the game.

If, in advancing, the base runner thinks there is a play and he slides past the base before or after touching it he may be put out by the fielder tagging him. If he fails to touch the base to which he is entitled and attempts to advance beyond that base he may be put out by tagging him or the base he missed.

(b) He is touched by a pitched ball which he is not attempting to hit unless (1) The ball is in the strike zone when it touches the batter, or (2) The batter makes no attempt to avoid being touched by the ball;

If the ball is in the strike zone when it touches the batter, it shall be called a strike, whether or not the batter tries to avoid the ball. If the ball is outside the strike zone when it touches the batter, it shall be called a ball if he makes no attempt to avoid being touched.

APPROVED RULING: When the batter is touched by a pitched ball which does not entitle him to first base, the ball is dead and no runner may advance.

(c) The catcher or any fielder interferes with him. If a play follows the interference, the manager of the offense may advise the plate umpire that he elects to decline the interference penalty and accept the play. Such election shall be made immediately at the end of the play. However, if the batter reaches first base on a hit, an error, a base on balls, a hit batsman, or otherwise, and all other runners advance at least one base, the play proceeds without reference to the interference.

If catcher's interference is called with a play in progress the umpire will allow the play to continue because the manager may elect to take the play. If the batter-runner missed first base, or a runner misses his next base, he shall be considered as having reached the base, as stated in Note of Rule 7.04 (d).

Examples of plays the manager might elect to take:

1. Runner on third, one out, batter hits fly ball to the outfield on which the runner scores but catcher's interference was called. The offensive manager may elect to take the run and have batter called out or have runner remain at third and batter awarded first base.

2. Runner on second base. Catcher interferes with batter as he bunts ball fairly sending runner to third base. The manager may rather have runner on third base with an out on the play than have runners on second and first.

In situations where the manager wants the "interference" penalty to apply, the following interpretation shall be made of 6.08 (c):

If the catcher (or any fielder) interferes with the batter, the batter is awarded first base. If, on such interference a runner is trying to score by a steal or squeeze from third base, the ball is dead and the runner on third scores and batter is awarded first base. If the catcher interferes with the batter with no runners trying to score from third on a squeeze or steal, then the ball is dead, batter is awarded first base and runners who are forced to advance, do advance. Runners not attempting to steal or not forced to advance remain on the base they occupied at the time of the interference.

If the catcher interferes with the batter before the pitcher delivers the ball, it shall not be considered interference on the batter under Rule 6.08 (c). In such cases, the umpire shall call "Time" and the pitcher and batter start over from "scratch."

(d) A fair ball touches an umpire or a runner on fair territory before touching a fielder.

If a fair ball touches an umpire after having passed a fielder other than the pitcher, or having touched a fielder, including the pitcher, the ball is in play.

6.09 The batter becomes a runner when—

(a) He hits a fair ball;

(b) The third strike called by the umpire is not caught, providing (1) first base is unoccupied, or (2) first base is occupied with two out;

When a batter becomes a base runner on a third strike not caught by the catcher and starts for the dugout, or his position, and then realizes his situation and attempts the reach first base, he is not out unless he or first base is tagged before he reaches first base. If, however, he actually reaches the dugout or dugout steps, he may not then attempt to go to first base and shall be out.

(c) A fair ball, after having passed a fielder other than the pitcher, or after having been touched by a fielder, including the pitcher, shall touch an umpire or runner on fair territory;

(d) A fair ball passes over a fence or into the stands at a distance from home base of 250 feet or more. Such hit entitles the batter to a home run when he shall have touched all bases legally. A fair fly ball that passes out of the playing field at a point less than 250 feet from home base shall entitle the batter to advance to second base only;

(e) A fair ball, after touching the ground, bounds into the stands, or passes through, over or under a fence, or through or under a scoreboard, or through or under shrubbery, or vines on the fence, in which case the batter and the runners shall be entitled to advance two bases;

(f) Any fair ball which, either before or after touching the ground, passes through or under a fence, or through or under a scoreboard, or through any opening in the fence or scoreboard, or through or under shrubbery, or vines on the fence, or which sticks in a fence or scoreboard, in which case the batter and the runners shall be entitled to two bases;

(g) Any bounding fair ball is deflected by the fielder into the stands, or over or under a fence on fair or foul territory, in which case the batter and all runners shall be entitled to advance two bases;

(h) Any fair fly ball is deflected by the fielder into the stands, or over the fence into foul territory, in which case the batter shall be entitled to advance to second base; but if deflected into the stands or over the fence in fair territory, the batter shall be entitled to a home run. However, should such a fair fly be deflected at a point less than 250 feet from home plate, the batter shall be entitled to two bases only.

6.10 Any League may elect to use the Designated Hitter Rule.

(a) In the event of inter-league competition between clubs of Leagues using the Designated Hitter Rule and clubs of Leagues not using the Designated Hitter Rule, the rule will be used as follows:

1. In exhibition games, the rule will be used or not used as is the practice of the home team.
2. In All-Star games, the rule will only be used if both teams and both Leagues so agree.
3. In World Series play the rule will be used every other year. It will not be used in 1977, but will be used in 1978, etc.

(b) The Rule provides as follows:

A hitter may be designated to bat for the starting pitcher and all subsequent pitchers in any game without otherwise affecting the status of the pitcher(s) in the game. A Designated Hitter for the pitcher must be selected prior to the game and must be included in the lineup cards presented to the Umpire in Chief.

The designated hitter named in the starting lineup must come to bat at least one time, unless the opposing club changes pitchers.

It is not mandatory that a club designate a hitter for the pitcher, but failure to do so prior to the game precludes the use of a Designated Hitter for that game.

Pinch hitters for a Designated Hitter may be used. Any substitute hitter for a Designated Hitter becomes the Designated Hitter. A replaced Designated Hitter shall not re-enter the game in any capacity.

The Designated Hitter may be used defensively, continuing to bat in the same position in the batting order, but the pitcher must then bat in the place of the substituted defensive player, unless more than one substitution is made, and the manager then must designate their spots in the batting order.

A runner may be substituted for the Designated Hitter and the runner assumes the role of Designated Hitter. A Designated Hitter may not pinch run.

A Designated Hitter is "locked" into the batting order. No multiple substitutions may be made that will alter the batting rotation of the Designated Hitter.

Once the game pitcher is switched from the mound to a defensive position this move shall terminate the Designated Hitter role for the remainder of the game.

Once a pinch hitter bats for any player in the batting order and then enters the game to pitch, this move shall terminate the Designated Hitter role for the remainder of the game.

Once the game pitcher bats for the Designated Hitter this move shall terminate the Designated Hitter role for the remainder of the game. (The game pitcher may only pinch-hit for the Designated Hitter).

Once a Designated Hitter assumes a defensive position this move shall terminate the Designated Hitter role for the remainder of the game. A substitute for the Designated Hitter need not be announced until it is the Designated Hitter's turn to bat.

7.00—The Runner.

7.01 A runner acquires the right to an unoccupied base when he touches it before he is out. He is then entitled to it until he is put out, or forced to vacate it for another runner legally entitled to that base.

If a runner legally acquires title to a base, and the pitcher assumes his pitching position, the runner may not return to a previously occupied base.

7.02 In advancing, a runner shall touch first, second, third and home base in order. If forced to return, he shall retouch all bases in reverse order, unless the ball is dead under any provision of Rule 5.09. In such cases, the runner may go directly to his original base.

7.03 Two runners may not occupy a base, but if, while the ball is alive, two runners are touching a base, the following runner shall be out when tagged. The preceding runner is entitled to the base.

7.04 Each runner, other than the batter, may without liability to be put out, advance one base when—

(a) There is a balk;

(b) The batter's advance without liability to be put out forces the runner to vacate his base, or when the batter hits a fair ball that touches another runner or the umpire before such ball has been touched by, or has passed a fielder, if the runner is forced to advance;

A runner forced to advance without liability to be put out may advance past the base to which he is entitled only at his peril. If such a runner, forced to advance, is put out for the third out before a preceding runner, also forced to advance, touches home plate, the run shall score.

Play. Two out, bases full, batter walks but runner from second is over-zealous and runs past third base toward home and is tagged out on a throw by the catcher. Even though two are out, the run would score on the theory that the run was forced home by the base on balls and that all the runners needed to do was proceed and touch the next base.

(c) A fielder, after catching a fly ball, falls into a bench or stand, or falls across ropes into a crowd when spectators are on the field;

A fielder or catcher may reach or step into, or go into the dugout with one or both feet to make a catch, and if he holds the ball, the catch shall be allowed. Ball is in play.

If the fielder or catcher, after having made a legal catch, should fall into a stand or among spectators or into the dugout after making a legal catch, or fall while in the dugout after making a legal catch, the ball is dead and runners advance one base without liability to be put out.

(d) While he is attempting to steal a base, the batter is interfered with by the catcher or any other fielder.

NOTE: When a runner is entitled to a base without liability to be put out, while the ball is in play, or under any rule in which the ball is in play after the runner reaches the base to which he is entitled, and the runner fails to touch the base to which he is entitled before attempting to advance to the next base, the runner shall forfeit his exemption from liability to be put out, and he may be put out by tagging the base or by tagging the runner befoe he returns to the missed base.

7.05 Each runner including the batter-runner may, without liability to be put out, advance—

(a) To home base, scoring a run, if a fair ball goes out of the playing field in flight and he touches all bases legally; or if a fair ball which, in the umpire's judgment, would have gone out of the playing field in flight, is deflected by the act of a fielder in throwing his glove, cap, or any article of his apparel;

(b) Three bases, if a fielder deliberately touches a fair ball with his cap, mask or any part of his uniform detached from its proper place on his person. The ball is in play and the batter may advance to home base at his peril;

(c) Three bases, if a fielder deliberately throws his glove at and touches a fair ball. The ball is in play and the batter may advance to home base at his peril.

(d) Two bases, if a fielder deliberately touches a thrown ball with his cap, mask or any part of his uniform detached from its proper place on his person. The ball is in play;

(e) Two bases, if a fielder deliberately throws his glove at and touches a thrown ball. The ball is in play;

In applying (b-c-d-e) the umpire must rule that the thrown glove or detached cap or mask has touched the ball. There is no penalty if the ball is not touched.

Under (c-e) this penalty shall not be invoked against a fielder whose glove is carried off his hand by the force of a batted or thrown ball, or when his glove flies off his hand as he makes an obvious effort to make a legitimate catch.

(f) Two bases, if a fair ball bounces or is deflected into the stands outside the first or third base foul lines; or if it goes through or under a field fence, or through or under a scoreboard, or through or under shrubbery or vines on the fence; or if it sticks in such fence, scoreboard, shrubbery or vines;

(g) Two bases when, with no spectators on the playing field, a thrown ball goes into the stands, or into a bench (whether or not the ball rebounds into the field), or over or under or through a field fence, or on a slanting part of the screen above the backstop, or remains in the meshes of a wire screen protecting spectators. The ball is dead. When such wild throw is the first play by an infielder, the umpire, in awarding such bases, shall be governed by the position of the runners at the time the ball was pitched; in all other cases the umpire shall be governed by the position of the runners at the time the wild throw was made;

APPROVED RULING: If all runners, including the batter-runner, have advanced at least one base when an infielder makes a wild throw on the first play after the pitch, the award shall be governed by the position of the runners when the wild throw was made.

In certain circumstances it is impossible to award a runner two bases. Example: Runner on first. Batter hits fly to short right. Runner holds up between first and second and batter comes around first and pulls up behind him. Ball falls safely. Outfielder, in throwing to first, throws ball into stand.

APPROVED RULING: Since no runner, when the ball is dead, may advance beyond the base to which he is entitled, the runner originally on first base goes to third base and the batter is held at second base.

The term "when the wild throw was made" means when the throw actually left the player's hand and not when the thrown ball hit the ground, passes a receiving fielder or goes out of play into the stands.

The position of the batter-runner at the time the wild throw left the thrower's hand is the key in deciding the award of bases. If the batter-runner has not reached first base, the award is two bases at the time the pitch was made for all runners. The decision as to whether the batter-runner has reached first base before the throw is a judgment call.

If an unusual play arises where a first throw by an infielder goes into stands or dugout but the batter did not become a runner (such as catcher throwing ball into stands in attempt to get runner from third trying to score on passed ball or wild pitch) award of two bases shall be from the position of the runners at the time of the throw. (For the purpose of Rule 7.05 (g) a catcher is considered an infielder.)

PLAY. Runner on first base, batter hits a ball to the shortstop, who throws to second base too late to get runner at second, and second baseman throws toward first base after batter has crossed first base. Ruling—Runner at second scores. (On this play, only if batter-runner is past first base when throw is made is he awarded third base.)

(h) One base, if a ball, pitched to the batter, or thrown by the pitcher from his position on the pitcher's plate to a base to catch a runner, goes into a stand or a bench, or over or through a field fence or backstop. The ball is dead;

APPROVED RULING: When a wild pitch or passed ball goes through or by the catcher, or deflects off the catcher, and goes directly into the dugout, stands, above the break, or any area where the ball is dead, the awarding of bases shall be one base. One base shall also be awarded if the pitcher while in contact with the rubber, throws to a base, and the throw goes directly into the stands or into any area where the ball is dead.

If, however, the pitched or thrown ball goes through or by the catcher or through the fielder, and remains on the playing field, and is subsequently kicked or deflected into the dugout, stands or other area where the ball is dead, the awarding of bases shall be two bases from position of runners at the time of the pitch or throw.

(i) One base, if the batter becomes a runner on Ball Four or Strike Three, when the pitch passes the catcher and lodges in the umpire's mask or paraphernalia.

If the batter becomes a runner on a wild pitch which entitles the runners to advance one base, the batter-runner shall be entitled to first base only.

The fact a runner is awarded a base or bases without liability to be put out does not relieve him of the responsibility to touch the base he is awarded and all intervening bases. For example: batter hits a ground ball which an infielder throws into the stands but the batter-runner missed first base. He may be called out on appeal for missing first base after the ball is put in play even though he was "awarded" second base.

If a runner is forced to return to a base after a catch, he must retouch his original base even though, because of some ground rule or other rule, he is awarded additional bases. He may retouch while the ball is dead and the award is then made from his original base.

7.06 When obstruction occurs, the umpire shall call or signal "Obstruction."

(a) If a play is being made on the obstructed runner, or if the batter-runner is obstructed before he touches first base, the ball is dead and all runners shall advance, without liability to be put out, to the bases they would have reached, in the umpire's judgment, if there had been no obstruction. The obstructed runner shall be awarded at least one base beyond the base he had last legally touched before the obstruction. Any preceding runners, forced to advance by the award of bases as the penalty for obstruction, shall advance without liability to be put out.

When a play is being made on an obstructed runner, the umpire shall signal obstruction in the same manner that he calls "Time," with both hands overhead. The ball is immediately dead when this signal is given; however, should a thrown ball be in flight before the obstruction is called by the umpire, the runners are to be awarded such bases on wild throws as they would have been awarded had no obstruction occurred. On a play where a runner was trapped between second and third base and obstructed by the third baseman going into third base while the throw is in flight from the shortstop, if such throw goes into the dugout the obstructed runner is to be awarded home base. Any other runners on base in this situation would also be awarded two bases from the base they last legally touched before obstruction was called.

(b) If no play is being made on the obstructed runner, the play shall proceed until no further action is possible. The umpire shall then call "Time" and impose such penalties, if any, as in his judgment will nullify the act of obstruction.

Under 7.06 (b) when the ball is not dead on obstruction and an obstructed runner advances beyond the base which, in the umpire's judgment, he would have been awarded because of being obstructed, he does so at his own peril and may be tagged out. This is a judgment call.

NOTE: The catcher, without the ball in his possession, has no right to block the pathway of the runner attempting to score. The base line belongs to the runner and the catcher should be there only when he is fielding a ball or when he already has the ball in his hand.

7.07 If, with a runner on third base and trying to score by means of a squeeze play or a steal, the catcher or any other fielder steps on, or in front of home base without possession of the ball, or touches the batter or his bat, the pitcher shall be charged with a balk, the batter shall be awarded first base on the interference and the ball is dead.

7.08 Any runner is out when—

(a) (1) He runs more than three feet away from a direct line between bases to avoid being tagged, unless his action is to avoid interference with a fielder fielding a batted ball; or (2) after touching first base, he leaves the baseline, obviously abandoning his effort to touch the next base;

Any runner after reaching first base who leaves the baseline heading for his dugout or his position believing that there is no further play, may be declared out if the umpire judges the act of the runner to be considered abandoning his efforts to run the bases. Even though an out is called, the ball remains in play in regard to any other runner.

This rule also covers the following and similar plays: Less than two out, score tied last of ninth inning, runner on first, batter hits a ball out of park for winning run, the runner on first passes second and thinking the home run automatically wins the game, cuts across diamond toward his bench as batter-runner circles bases. In this case, the base runner would be called out "for abandoning his effort to touch the next base" and batter-runner permitted to continue around bases to make his home run valid. If there are two out, home run would not count (see Rule 7.12). This is not an appeal play.

PLAY. Runner believing he is called out on a tag at first or third base starts for the dugout and progresses a reasonable distance still indicating by his actions that he is out, shall be declared out for abandoning the bases.

In the above two plays the runners are considered actually abandoning their base paths and are treated differently than the batter who struck out as described. APPROVED RULING OF 7.08 (a).

APPROVED RULING: When a batter becomes a runner on third strike not caught, and starts for his bench or position, he may advance to first base at any time before he enters the bench. To put him out, the defense must tag him or first base before he touches first base.

(b) He intentionally interferes with a thrown ball; or hinders a fielder attempting to make a play on a batted ball;

A runner who is adjudged to have hindered a fielder who is attempting to make a play on a batted ball is out whether it was intentional or not.

If, however, the runner has contact with a legally occupied base when he hinders the fielder, he shall not be called out unless, in the umpire's judgment, such hindrance, whether it occurs on fair or foul territory, is intentional. If the umpire declares the hindrance intentional, the following penalty shall apply: With less than two out, the umpire shall declare both the runner and batter out. With two out, the umpire shall declare the batter out.

If, in a run-down between third base and home plate, the succeeding runner has advanced and is standing on third base when the runner in a run-down is called out for offensive interference, the umpire shall send the runner standing on third base back to second base. This same principle applies if there is a run-down between second and third base and succeeding runner has reached second (the reasoning is that no runner shall advance on an interference play and a runner is considered to occupy a base until he legally has reached the next succeeding base).

(c) He is tagged, when the ball is alive, while off his base. EXCEPTION: A batter-runner cannot be tagged out after overrunning or oversliding first base if he returns immediately to the base;

APPROVED RULING: (1) If the impact of a runner breaks a base loose from its position, no play can be made on that runner at that base if he had reached the base safely.

APPROVED RULING: (2) If a base is dislodged from its position during a play, any following runner on the same play shall be considered as touching or occupying the base if, in the umpire's judgment, he touches or occupies the point marked by the dislodged bag.

(d) He fails to retouch his base after a fair or foul ball is legally caught before he, or his base, is tagged by a fielder. He shall not be called out for failure to retouch his base after the first following pitch, or any play or attempted play. This is an appeal play;

Runners need not "tag up" on a foul tip. They may steal on a foul tip. If a so-called tip is not caught, it becomes an ordinary foul. Runners then return to their bases.

(e) He fails to reach the next base before a fielder tags him or the base, after he has been forced to advance by reason of the batter becoming a runner. However, if a following runner is put out on a force play, the force is removed and the runner must be tagged to be put out. The force is removed as soon as the runner touches the base to which he is forced to advance, and if he overslides or overruns the base, the runner must be tagged to be put out. However, if the forced runner, after touching the next base, retreats for any reason towards the base he had last occupied, the force play is reinstated, and he can again be put out if the defense tags the base to which he is forced;

PLAY. Runner on first and three balls on batter: Runner steals on the next pitch, which is fourth ball, but after having touched second he overslides or overruns that base. Catcher's throw catches him before he can return. Ruling is that runner is out. (Force out is removed.)

Oversliding and overrunning situations arise at bases other than first base. For instance, before two are out, and runners on first and second, or first, second and third, the ball is hit to an infielder who tries for the double play. The runner on first beats the throw to second base but overslides the base. The relay is made to first base and the batter-runner is out. The first baseman, seeing the runner at second base off the bag, makes the return throw to second and the runner is tagged off the base. Meanwhile runners have crossed the plate. The question is: Is this a force play? Was the force removed when the batter-runner was out at first base? Do the runs that crossed the plate during this play and before the third out was made when the runner was tagged at second, count? Answer: The runs score. It is not a force play. It is a tag play.

(f) He is touched by a fair ball in fair territory before the ball has touched or passed an infielder. The ball is dead and no runner may score, nor runners advance, except runners forced to advance. EXCEPTION: If a runner is touching his base when touched by an Infield Fly, he is not out, although the batter is out;

If two runners are touched by the same fair ball, only the first one is out because the ball is instantly dead.

If runner is touched by an Infield Fly when he is not touching his base, both runner and batter are out.

(g) He attempts to score on a play in which the batter interferes with the play at home base before two are out. With two out, the interference puts the batter out and no score counts;

(h) He passes a preceding runner before such runner is out;

(i) After he has acquired legal possession of a base, he runs the bases in reverse order for the purpose of confusing the defense or making a travesty of the game. The umpire shall immediately call "Time" and declare the runner out;

If a runner touches an unoccupied base and then thinks the ball was caught or is decoyed into returning to the base he last touched, he may be put out running back to that base, but if he reaches the previously occupied base safely he cannot be put out while in contact with that base.

(j) He fails to return at once to first base after overrunning or oversliding that base. If he attempts to run to second he is out when tagged. If, after overrunning or oversliding first base he starts toward the dugout, or toward his position, and fails to return to first base at once, he is out, on appeal, when he or the base is tagged;

Runner who touches first base in overrunning and is declared safe by the umpire has, within the intent of Rule 4.09 (a) "reached first base" and any run which scores on such a play counts, even though the runner subsequently becomes the third out for failure to return "at once," as covered in Rule 7.08 (j).

(k) In running or sliding for home base, he fails to touch home base and makes no attempt to return to the base, when a fielder holds the ball in his hand, while touching home base, and appeals to the umpire for the decision.

This rule applies only where runner is on his way to the bench and the catcher would be required to chase him. It does not apply to the ordinary play where the runner misses the plate and then immediately makes an effort to touch the plate before being tagged. In that case, runner must be tagged.

7.09 It is interference by a batter or a runner when—

(a) After a third strike he hinders the catcher in his attempt to field the ball;

(b) After hitting or bunting a fair ball, his bat hits the ball a second time in fair territory. The ball is dead and no runners may advance. If the batter-runner drops his bat and the ball rolls against the bat in fair territory and, in the umpire's judgment, there was no intention to interfere with the course of the ball, the ball is alive and in play;

(c) He intentionally deflects the course of a foul ball in any manner;

(d) Before two are out and a runner on third base, the batter hinders a fielder in making a play at home base; the runner is out;

(e) **Any member or members of the offensive team stand or gather around any base to which a runner is advancing, to confuse, hinder or add to the difficulty of the fielders. Such runner shall** be declared out for the interference of his teammate or teammates;

(f) Any batter or runner who has just been put out hinders or impedes any following play being made on a runner. Such runner shall be declared out for the interference of his teammate;

If the batter or a runner continues to advance after he has been put out, he shall not by that act alone be considered as confusing, hindering or impeding the fielders.

(g) If, in the judgment of the umpire, a base runner wilfully and deliberately interferes with a batted ball or a fielder in the act of fielding a batted ball with the obvious intent to break up a double play, the ball is dead. The umpire shall call the runner out for interference and also call out the batter-runner because of the action of his teammate. In no event may bases be run or runs scored because of such action by a runner.

(h) If, in the judgment of the umpire, a batter-runner wilfully and deliberately interferes with a batted ball or a fielder in the act of fielding a batted ball, with the obvious intent to break up a double play, the ball is dead; the umpire shall call the batter-runner out for interference and shall also call out the runner who had advanced closest to the home plate regardless where the double play might have been possible. In no event shall bases be run because of such interference.

(i) In the judgment of the umpire, the base coach at third base, or first base, by touching or holding the runner, physically assists him in returning to or leaving third base or first base.

(j) With a runner on third base, the base coach leaves his box and acts in any manner to draw a throw by a fielder;

(k) In running the last half of the distance from home base to first base while the ball is being fielded to first base, he runs outside (to the right of) the three-foot line, or inside (to the left of) the foul line and, in the umpire's judgment, interferes with the fielder taking the throw at first base, or attempting to field a batted ball;

The lines marking the three foot lane are a part of that "lane" but the interpretation to be made is that a runner is required to have both feet within the three foot "lane" or on the lines marking the "lane."

(l) He fails to avoid a fielder who is attempting to field a batted ball, or intentionally interferes with a thrown ball, provided that if two or more fielders attempt to field a batted ball, and the runner comes in contact with one or more of them, the umpire shall determine which fielder is entitled to the benefit of this rule, and shall not declare the runner out for coming in contact with a fielder other than the one the umpire determines to be entitled to field such a ball;

When a catcher and batter-runner going to first base have contact when the catcher is fielding the ball, there is generally no violation and nothing should be called. "Obstruction" by a fielder attempting to field a ball should be called only in very flagrant and violent cases because the rules give him the right of way, but of course such "right of way" is not a license to, for example, intentionally trip a runner even though fielding the ball. If the catcher is fielding the ball and the first baseman or pitcher obstructs a runner going to first base "obstruction" shall be called and the base runner awarded first base.

(m) A fair ball touches him on fair territory before touching a fielder. If a fair ball goes through, or by, an infielder, and touches a runner immediately back of him, or touches the runner after having been deflected by a fielder, the umpire shall not declare the runner out for being touched by a batted ball. In making such decision the umpire must be convinced that the ball passed through, or by, the fielder, and that no other infielder had the chance to make a play on the ball. If, in the judgment of the umpire, the runner deliberately and intentionally kicks such a batted ball on which the infielder has missed a play, then the runner shall be called out for interference.

PENALTY FOR INTERFERENCE. The runner is out and the ball is dead.

7.10 Any runner shall be called out, on appeal, when—

(a) After a fly ball is caught, he fails to retouch his original base before he or his original base is tagged;

"Retouch," in this rule, means to tag up and start from a contact with the base after the ball is caught. A runner is not permitted to take a flying start from a position in back of his base.

(b) With the ball in play, while advancing or returning to a base, he fails to touch each base in order before he, or a missed base, is tagged.

APPROVED RULING: (1) No runner may return to touch a missed base after a following runner has scored. (2) When the ball is dead, no runner may return to touch a missed base or one he has left after he has advanced to and touched a base beyond the missed base.

PLAY. (a) Batter hits ball out of park or ground rule double and misses first base (ball is dead)—he may return to first base to correct his mistake before he touches second but if he touches second he may not return to first and if defensive team appeals he is declared out at first.

PLAY. (b) Batter hits ball to shortstop who throws wild into stand (ball is dead)—batter-runner misses first base but is awarded second base on the overthrow. Even though the umpire has awarded the runner second base on the overthrow, the runner must touch first base before he proceeds to second base.

These are appeal plays.

(c) He overruns or overslides first base and fails to return to the base immediately, and he or the base is tagged;

(d) He fails to touch home base and makes no attempt to return to that base, and home base is tagged.

Any appeal under this rule must be made before the next pitch, or any play or attempted play. If the violation occurs during a play which ends a half-inning, the appeal must be made before the defensive team leaves the field.

An appeal is not to be interpreted as a play or an attempted play.

Successive appeals may not be made on a runner at the same base. If the defensive team on its first appeal errs, a request for a second appeal on the same runner at the same base shall not be allowed by the umpire. (Intended meaning of the word "err" is that the defensive team in making an appeal threw the ball out of play. For example, if the pitcher threw to first base to appeal and threw the ball into the stands, no second appeal would be allowed.)

Appeal plays may require an umpire to recognize an apparent "fourth out." If the third out is made during a play in which an appeal play is sustained on another runner, the appeal play decision takes precedence in determining the out. If there is more than one appeal during a play that ends a half-inning, the defense may elect to take the out that gives it the advantage. For the purpose of this rule, the defensive team has "left the field" when the pitcher and all infielders have left fair territory on their way to the bench or clubhouse.

If two runners arrive at home base about the same time and the first runner misses home base but a second runner legally touches the plate, the first runner will be called out on appeal. If there are two out, and the first runner is tagged out on his attempt to come back and touch the base or is called out, on appeal, then he shall be considered as having been put out before the second runner scored and being the third out. Second runner's run shall not count, as provided in Rule 7.12.

If a pitcher balks when making an appeal, such act shall be a play. An appeal should be clearly intended as an appeal, either by a verbal request by the player or an act that unmistakably indicates an appeal to the umpire. A player, inadvertently stepping on the base with a ball in his hand, would not constitute an appeal. Time is not out when an appeal is being made.

7.11 The players, coaches or any member of an offensive team shall vacate any space (including both dugouts) needed by a fielder who is attempting to field a batted or thrown ball.

PENALTY: Interference shall be called and the batter or runner on whom the play is being made shall be declared out.

7.12 Unless two are out, the status of a following runner is not affected by a preceding runner's failure to touch or retouch a base. If, upon appeal, the preceding runner is the third out, no runners following him shall score. If such third out is the result of a force play, neither preceding nor following runners shall score.

8.00—The Pitcher.

8.01 Legal pitching delivery. There are two legal pitching positions, the Windup Position and the Set Position, and either position may be used at any time.

Pitchers shall take signs from the catcher while standing on the rubber.

Pitchers may disengage the rubber after taking their signs but may not step quickly onto the rubber and pitch. This may be judged a quick pitch by the umpire. When the pitcher disengages the rubber, he must drop his hands to his sides.

Pitchers will not be allowed to disengage the rubber after taking each sign.

(a) The Windup Position. The pitcher shall stand facing the batter, his entire pivot foot on, or in front of and touching and not off the end of the pitcher's plate, and the other foot free. From this position any natural movement associated with his delivery of the ball to the batter commits him to the pitch without interruption or alteration. He shall not raise either foot from the ground, except that in his actual delivery of the ball to the batter, he may take one step backward, and one step forward with his free foot.

When a pitcher holds the ball with both hands in front of his body, with his entire pivot foot on, or in front of and touching but not off the end of the pitcher's plate, and his other foot free, he will be considered in the Windup Position.

The pitcher may have one foot, not the pivot foot, off the rubber and any distance he may desire back of a line which is an extension to the back edge of the pitcher's plate, but not at either side of the pitcher's plate.

With his "free" foot the pitcher may take one step backward and one step forward, but under no circumstances, to either side, that is to either the first base or third base side of the pitcher's rubber.

If a pitcher holds the ball with both hands in front of his body, with his entire pivot foot on or in front of and touching but not off the end of the pitcher's plate, and his other foot free, he will be considered in a windup position.

From this position he may:

(1) deliver the ball to the batter, or

(2) step and throw to a base in an attempt to pick-off a runner, or

(3) disengage the rubber (if he does he must drop his hands to his sides).

In disengaging the rubber the pitcher must step off with his pivot foot and not his free foot first.

He may not go into a set or stretch position—if he does it is a balk.

(b) The Set Position. Set Position shall be indicated by the pitcher when he stands facing the batter with his entire pivot foot on, or in front of, and in contact with, and not off the end of the pitcher's plate, and his other foot in front of the pitcher's plate, holding the ball in both hands in front of his body and coming to a complete stop. From such Set Position he may deliver the ball to the batter, throw to a base or step backward off the pitcher's plate with his pivot foot. Before assuming Set Position, the pitcher may elect to make any natural preliminary motion such as that known as "the stretch." But if he so elects, he shall come to Set Position before delivering the ball to the batter. After assuming Set Position, any natural motion associated with his delivery of the ball to the batter commits him to the pitch without alteration or interruption.

Preparatory to coming to a set position, the pitcher shall have one hand on his side; from this position he shall go to his set position as defined in Rule 8.01 (b) without interruption and in one continuous motion.

The whole width of the foot in contact with the rubber must be on the rubber. A pitcher cannot pitch from off the end of the rubber with just the side of his foot touching the rubber.

The pitcher, following his stretch, must (a) hold the ball in both hands in front of his body and (b) come to a complete stop. This must be enforced. Umpires should watch this closely. Pitchers are constantly attempting to "beat the rule" in their efforts to hold runners on bases and in cases where the pitcher fails to make a complete "stop" called for in the rules, the umpire should immediately call a "Balk."

(c) At any time during the pitcher's preliminary movements and until his natural pitching motion commits him to the pitch, he may throw to any base provided he steps directly toward such base before making the throw.

The pitcher shall step "ahead of the throw." A snap throw followed by the step directly toward the base is a balk.

(d) If the pitcher makes an illegal pitch with the bases unoccupied, it shall be call a ball unless the batter reaches first base on a hit, an error, a base on balls, a hit batter or otherwise.

A ball which slips out of a pitcher's hand and crosses the foul line shall be called a ball; otherwise it will be called no pitch. This would be a balk with men on base.

(e) If the pitcher removes his pivot foot from contact with the pitcher's plate by stepping backward with that foot, he thereby becomes an infielder and if he makes a wild throw from that position, it shall be considered the same as a wild throw by any other infielder.

The pitcher, while off the rubber, may throw to any base. If he makes a wild throw, such throw is the throw of an infielder and what follows is governed by the rules covering a ball thrown by a fielder.

8.02 The pitcher shall not—

(a) (1) Bring his pitching hand in contact with his mouth or lips while in the 18 foot circle surrounding the pitching rubber. EXCEPTION: Provided it is agreed to by both managers, the umpire prior to the start of a game played in cold weather, may permit the pitcher to blow on his hand.
PENALTY: For violation of this part of this rule the umpires shall immediately call a ball. However, if the pitch is made and a batter reaches first base on a hit, an error, a hit batsman or otherwise, and no other runner is put out before advancing at least one base, the play shall proceed without reference to the violation. Repeated offenders shall be subject to a fine by the league president.

(2) Apply a foreign substance of any kind to the ball;

(3) expectorate on the ball, either hand or his glove;

(4) rub the ball on his glove, person or clothing;

(5) deface the ball in any manner;

(6) deliver what is called the "shine" ball, "spit" ball, "mud" ball or "emery" ball. The pitcher, of course, is allowed to rub the ball between his bare hands.
PENALTY: For violation of any part of this rule 8.02 (a) (2 to 6) the umpire shall:

(a) Call the pitch a ball, warn the pitcher and have announced on the public address system the reason for the action.

(b) In the case of a second offense by the same pitcher in the same game, the pitcher shall be disqualified from the game.

(c) If a play follows the violation called by the umpire, the manager of the offense may advise the plate umpire that he elects to accept the play. Such election shall be made immediately at the end of the play. However, if the batter reaches first base on a hit, an error, a base on balls, a hit batsman, or otherwise, and no other runner is put out before advancing at least one base, the play shall proceed without reference to the violation.

(d) Even though the offense elects to take the play, the violation shall be recognized and the penalties in (a) and (b) will still be in effect.

(e) The umpire shall be sole judge on whether any portion of this rule has been violated.

All umpires shall carry with them one official rosin bag. The umpire-in-chief is responsible for placing the rosin bag on the ground back of the pitcher's plate. If at any time the ball hits the rosin bag it is in play. In the case of rain or wet field, the umpire may instruct the pitcher to carry the rosin bag in his hip pocket. A pitcher may use the rosin bag for the purpose of applying rosin to his bare hand or hands. Neither the pitcher nor any other player shall dust the ball with the rosin bag; neither shall the pitcher nor any other player be permitted to apply rosin from the bag to his glove or dust any part of his uniform with the rosin bag.

(b) Have on his person, or in his possession, any foreign substance. For such infraction of this section (b) the penalty shall be immediate ejection from the game.

(c) Intentionally delay the game by throwing the ball to players other than the catcher, when the batter is in position, except in an attempt to retire a runner.
PENALTY: If, after warning by the umpire, such delaying action is repeated, the pitcher shall be removed from the game.

(d) Intentionally Pitch at the Batter.

If, in the umpire's judgment, such a violation occurs, the umpire shall warn the pitcher and his manager that another such pitch will mean immediate expulsion of the pitcher. At the same time the umpire shall warn the opposing manager that such an infraction by his pitcher shall result in that pitcher's expulsion.

If, in the umpire's judgment, there is another such pitch during the game by any pitcher, the umpire shall eject the pitcher from the game.

If, in the umpire's judgment, circumstances warrant, one or both teams may be officially "warned" prior to the game or an actual violation during the game in progress.

(League Presidents may take additional action.)

To pitch at a batter's head is unsportsmanlike and highly dangerous. It should be—and is—condemned by everybody. Umpires should act without hesitation in enforcement of this rule.

8.03 When a pitcher takes his position at the beginning of each inning, or when he relieves another pitcher, he shall be permitted to pitch not to exceed eight preparatory pitches to his catcher during which play shall be suspended. A league by its own action may limit the number of preparatory pitches to less than eight preparatory pitches. Such preparatory pitches shall not consume more than one minute of time. If a sudden emergency causes a pitcher to be summoned into the game without any opportunity to warm up, the umpire-in-chief shall allow him as many pitches as the umpire deems necessary.

8.04 When the bases are unoccupied, the pitcher shall deliver the ball to the batter within 20 seconds after he receives the ball. Each time the pitcher delays the game by violating this rule, the umpire shall call "Ball."

The intent of this rule is to avoid unnecessary delays. The umpire shall insist that the catcher return the ball promptly to the pitcher, and that the pitcher take his position on the rubber promptly. Obvious delay by the pitcher should instantly be penalized by the umpire.

8.05 If there is a runner, or runners, it is a balk when—

(a) The pitcher, while touching his plate, makes any motion naturally associated with his pitch and fails to make such delivery;

If a lefthanded or righthanded pitcher swings his free foot past the back edge of the pitcher's rubber, he is required to pitch to the batter except to throw to second base on a pick-off play.

(b) The pitcher, while touching his plate, feints a throw to first base and fails to complete the throw;

(c) The pitcher, while touching his plate, fails to step directly toward a base before throwing to that base;

Requires the pitcher, while touching his plate, to step directly toward a base before throwing to that base. If a pitcher turns or spins off of his free foot without actually stepping or if he turns his body and throws before stepping, it is a balk.

A pitcher is to step directly toward a base before throwing to that base but does not require him to throw (except to first base only) because he steps. It is possible, with runners on first and third, for the pitcher to step toward third and not throw, merely to bluff the runner back to third; then seeing the runner on first start for second, turn and step toward and throw to first base. This is legal. However, if, with runners on first and third, the pitcher, while in contact with the rubber, steps toward third and then immediately and in practically the same motion "wheels" and throws to first base, it is obviously an attempt to deceive the runner at first base, and in such a move it is practically impossible to step directly toward first base before the throw to first base, and such a move shall be called a balk. Of course, if the pitcher steps off the rubber and then makes such a move, it is not a balk.

(d) The pitcher, while touching his plate, throws, or feints a throw to an unoccupied base, except for the purpose of making a play;

(e) The pitcher makes an illegal pitch;

A quick pitch is an illegal pitch. Umpires will judge a quick pitch as one delivered before the batter is reasonably set in the batter's box. With runners on base the penalty is a balk; with no runners on base, it is a ball. The quick pitch is dangerous and should not be permitted.

(f) The pitcher delivers the ball to the batter while he is not facing the batter;

(g) The pitcher makes any motion naturally associated with his pitch while he is not touching the pitcher's plate;

(h) The pitcher unnecessarily delays the game;

(i) The pitcher, without having the ball, stands on or astride the pitcher's plate or while off the plate, he feints a pitch;

(j) The pitcher, after coming to a legal pitching position, removes one hand from the ball other than in an actual pitch, or in throwing to a base;

(k) The pitcher, while touching his plate, accidentally or intentionally drops the ball;

(l) The pitcher, while giving an intentional base on balls, pitches when the catcher is not in the catcher's box;

(m) The pitcher delivers the pitch from Set Position without coming to a stop.

PENALTY: The ball is dead, and each runner shall advance one base without liability to be put out, unless the batter reaches first on a hit, an error, a base on balls, a hit batter, or otherwise, and all other runners advance at least one base, in which case the play proceeds without reference to the balk.

APPROVED RULING: In cases where a pitcher balks and throws wild, either to a base or to home plate, a runner or runners may advance beyond the base to which he is entitled at his own risk.

APPROVED RULING: A runner who misses the first base to which he is advancing and who is called out on appeal shall be considered as having advanced one base for the purpose of this rule.

Umpires should bear in mind that the purpose of the balk rule is to prevent the pitcher from deliberately deceiving the base runner. If there is doubt in the umpire's mind, the "intent" of the pitcher should govern. However, certain specifics should be borne in mind:

(a) Straddling the pitcher's rubber without the ball is to be interpreted as intent to deceive and ruled a balk.

(b) With a runner on first base the pitcher may make a complete turn, without hesitating toward first, and throw to second. This is not to be interpreted as throwing to an unoccupied base.

8.06 A professional league shall adopt the following rule pertaining to the visit of the manager or coach to the pitcher:

(a) This rule limits the number of trips a manager or coach may make to any one pitcher in any one inning; (b) A second trip to the same pitcher in the same inning will cause this pitcher's automatic removal; (c) The manager or coach is prohibited from making a second visit to the mound while the same batter is at bat, but (d) if a pinch-hitter is substituted for this batter, the manager or coach may make a second visit to the mound, but must remove the pitcher.

A manager or coach is considered to have concluded his visit to the mound when he leaves the 18-foot circle surrounding the pitcher's rubber.

If the manager or coach goes to the catcher or infielder and that player then goes to the mound or the pitcher comes to him at his position before there is an intervening play (a pitch or other play) that will be the same as the manager or coach going to the mound.

Any attempt to evade or circumvent this rule by the manager or coach going to the catcher or an infielder and then that player going to the mound to confer with the pitcher shall constitute a trip to the mound.

If the coach goes to the mound and removes a pitcher and then the manager goes to the mound to talk with the new pitcher, that will constitute one trip to that new pitcher that inning.

In a case where a manager has made his first trip to the mound and then returns the second time to the mound in the same inning with the same pitcher in the game and the same batter at bat, after being warned by the umpire that he cannot return to the mound, the manager shall be removed from the game and the pitcher required to pitch to the batter until he is retired or gets on base. After the batter is retired, or becomes a base runner, then this pitcher must be removed from the game. The manager should be notified that his pitcher will be removed from the game after he pitches to one hitter, so he can have a substitute pitcher warmed up.

The substitute pitcher will be allowed eight preparatory pitches or more if in the umpire's judgment circumstances justify.